Emilio Dicerbo

THE
BIRDWATCHERS
ALMANAC

Bloomsbury Books · London

First published by Lochar Publishing Ltd.
Moffat, Scotland DG10 9ED.

This edition published by Bloomsbury Books, an imprint of
The Godfrey Cave Group, 42 Bloomsbury Street, London, WC1B 3QJ,
under licence from Eric Dobby Publishing Ltd,
12 Warnford Road, Orpington, Kent BR6 6LW, 1993

Printed and bound in Great Britain by
BPCC Hazell Books Ltd

Member of BPCC Ltd

ISBN 1 85471 134 2

Contents

Credits

Introduction

The Birdwatchers Almanac includes descriptions of over 200 species, around half of which are illustrated in colour, and amongst these are residents, summer residents, winter visitors and passage migrants.

The size of each bird is given in comparison to a well-known species and where details of nests and eggs have been omitted this indicates that the species does not normally breed in the British Isles.

The birds are grouped under four habitat headings. In the case of residents and summer residents these groupings relate to where they can usually be found breeding, and in the case of winter visitors and passage migrants where they can be found feeding.

Emilio Dicerbo

1992

Comparative sizes of familiar species

Blue Tit = 11.5 cm

Starling = 21.5 cm

Lapwing = 30 cm

Buzzard = 54 cm

Mallard = 65 cm

<u>Comparative sizes of familiar species</u>

Chaffinch = 15 cm

Blackbird = 25 cm

Wood Pigeon = 40 cm

Herring Gull = 60 cm

Canada Goose = 95 cm

Birds of Gardens and Woodlands

Gardens provide nest sites for many species of birds, most of which are resident with us throughout the year, with Finches and Tits topping the list. In summer, outhouses may be occupied by nesting Swallows, nest-boxes by Fly-catchers and Redstarts, while House Martins may build under the eaves of house roofs. In larger gardens, Warblers may even take up residence.

In winter, gardens which provide food in the shape of seeds, berries, windfall fruit and well-stocked bird tables, will see the list of garden visitors greatly extended, and in addition to the regular visitors, gardens near woodlands may attract Woodpeckers, Nuthatches, Wrens, Jays and Magpies, while those situated near water may be visited by Wagtails and Moorhens. Even town gardens may receive visits from Fieldfares, Redwings, Bramblings and Waxwings during severe weather.

Most of the birds which are regular visitors to gardens in winter rear their young in nearby woodlands in spring, preferring open broad-leaved woodland where the habitat provides nest sites and food. Fortunately there are still substantial areas of such woodland in some parts of the country.

By no means as productive, the vast areas of closely planted conifers found in other parts of the country provide a habitat for a more restricted variety of species, whereas the natural, ancient pine forests of northern Scotland support a variety of species more closely aligned to areas of broad-leaved woodland.

Blackbird
Turdus merula

Blackbird

Size and Field Characteristics 25 cm.
A most familiar bird. Male in summer has all black
plumage, orange-yellow bill and yellow rim round eye.
Female is dark-brown with paler brown chin and breast
spotted with dark-brown. Immature birds show slight
variation in colouring.

Status
Resident.

Habitat and Range
Gardens, parkland, woodlands of all kinds throughout
Britain.

Nest
Cup-shaped, built with twigs, grasses, moss, mud and
fibres, situated at times on ground, but mostly one to
four metres above ground in a bush hedge or conifer.

Eggs
Bluish-green, speckled with reddish brown. Clutch 3-6.

Food
Blackbirds frequent lawns in their search for
earthworms, overturn dead leaves for spiders, centipedes
and grubs, pluck berries from bushes and trees and
accept all manner of kitchen scraps in winter.

Mistle Thrush
Turdus viscivorus

Mistle Thrush

Size and Field Characteristics   27 cm.
Larger than Blackbird. Largest of British Thrushes.
Brownish-grey upper-parts, white underwing and pale
breast with large dark-brown spots, white outer tail
feathers. Upright stance when seen on ground. Habit of
singing from high vantage point during spring storms
earns it the name of 'Storm Cock'.
Status
Resident.
Habitat and Range
Gardens, parkland, woodlands and open country
throughout British Isles.
Nest
Usually placed in tree fork or bush, at times
conspicuous, built with twigs, roots, grasses and moss.
Eggs
Bluish-green to creamy-brown with grey markings.
Clutch 3-5.
Food
Fruit, berries, earthworms and other invertebrates.

Song Thrush
Turdus philomelos

Song Thrush

Size and Field Characteristics   23 cm.
Smaller than Blackbird. A familiar garden songbird.
Brown upper-parts, pale throat and breast heavily
spotted with dark-brown, pale orange underwing seen in
flight. Characteristic listening pose when seen on lawns.
Status
Resident.
Habitat and Range
Gardens, parks, hedgerows and woodlands throughout
the British Isles. Many move south for winter.
Nest
Built in bush, hedge or tree, occasionally on ground,
made with twigs and grasses, lined with mud.
Eggs
Pale blue with black spots. Clutch 4-5.
Food
Worms, invertebrates, fruit. Song Thrushes carry snails
to a favourite stone called an 'anvil' where they crack
open the shells with their beaks to reach the slugs.

Fieldfare
Turdus pilaris

Fieldfare

Size and Field Characteristics 25.5 cm.
Slightly larger than Blackbird. Chestnut back and wings
with dark-brown outer feathers, tail also dark. Head and
rump grey, breast cream, heavily spotted, belly white,
white underwing. Characteristic 'chuk chuk' call heard
in flight.

Status
Mainly winter visitor, when they usually appear in large
numbers. Rare breeder.

Habitat and Range
Open country, hedgerows and parkland throughout the
British Isles from autumn to spring when they return to
Scandinavian and Icelandic breeding haunts. Rarely
breeds in the north of Scotland.

Nest
In tree fork, constructed with twigs and grasses.

Eggs
Greenish-blue, speckled with brown. Clutch 4-5.

Food
Worms, insects and berries. In severe frosty weather
they will peck at turnips.

Redwing
Turdus iliacus

Redwing

Size and Field Characteristics 21 cm.
Smaller than Blackbird. Brown upper-parts, pale, brown spotted throat and breast, conspicuous white eye-stripe, reddish flanks and underwing noticeable in flight. Often seen in the company of other Thrushes, especially Fieldfares.

Status
Mainly winter visitor, small resident population.

Habitat and Range
Open country, hedgerows, parks and gardens. Scandinavian and Icelandic Redwings roam the British Isles during winter, returning to their breeding haunts in Spring. Small resident population in northern half of Scotland.

Nest
Built with twigs and grasses in low bush or on the ground.

Eggs
Greenish, spotted with reddish-brown. Clutch 4-6.

Food
Worms, insects and berries. Many Redwings perish in severe frosty weather when berry crop is exhausted.

Chaffinch
Fringilla coelebs

Chaffinch

Size and Field Characteristics   15 cm.
Slightly larger than House Sparrow. Most common
British Finch. In summer, male has blue-grey crown and
nape; black, white and greenish wings; pink under-
parts; white outer tail feathers. In winter, male's crown
turns brown. Female is less colourful at all times.
Roams countryside in large flocks in winter, usually
accompanied by other Finches and Buntings.
Status
Resident.
Habitat and Range
Woodland, parkland and gardens throughout the British
Isles. Resident numbers greatly increased in winter by
birds from northern and eastern Europe.
Nest
A beautiful cup-shaped little structure of moss, lichen,
hair and feathers, built in fork of tree, hedge or conifer,
one to five metres from ground.
Eggs
Greyish-stone, slightly spotted and streaked with dark
reddish-brown. Clutch 4-5.
Food
Insects, caterpillars, seeds and grain. Constant visitor to
bird tables in winter.

Brambling
Fringilla montifringilla

Brambling

Size and Field Characteristics   14.5 cm.
Slightly smaller than Chaffinch. Often found in the
company of Chaffinches, a boldly marked Finch with
dark head and back, orange breast, white belly and
conspicuous white rump, this being best identification
feature when disturbed.

Status
Winter visitor. Rare breeder.

Habitat and Range
Widespread throughout British Isles in winter, absent
from extreme north-west Scotland. A breeding bird in
Scandinavia and eastern Europe. A few pairs may breed
in Scotland.

Food
Mainly beechmast and other seeds; in severe weather
gardens and bird tables are visited.

Greenfinch
Carduelis chloris

Greenfinch

Size and Field Characteristics   14.5 cm.
Slightly smaller than Chaffinch. Male has green
plumage, greyish wings with bright yellow patches,
bright yellow base to dark tail. Stout beak. Female's
plumage is browner with less prominent yellow flashes
on wings and tail.
Status
Resident.
Habitat and Range
Woodland edges, parkland, gardens and hedgerows
throughout British Isles except for north-west Scotland.
Nest
Greenfinches nest in loose colonies in rhododendrons,
yew trees, conifers, ivy and thick hedgerows. The nest
is built with twigs, moss, fibres and wool.
Eggs
Whitish with reddish-brown spots. Clutch 4-6.
Food
Seeds, grain, insects and berries. Greenfinches visit bird
tables in winter, their stout beaks tearing holes in
'Netlon' nut-holders in seconds.

Siskin
Carduelis spinus

Siskin

Size and Field Characteristics 12 cm.
Smaller than Chaffinch. A green and dark brown
streaked little bird, yellow rump and wing bars, short
forked tail. Male has black cap and bib. Female's
plumage is slightly duller and lacks male's black cap.
Agile Tit-like manner when feeding.

Status
Resident and winter visitor.

Habitat and Range
In summer, mainly conifer forests. In winter, birch and
alder woods also frequented. Found breeding
throughout most of Scotland, north of England and
central Wales.

Nest
Situated high in conifer, built with twigs, moss, lichens,
down and hair.

Eggs
Bluish with pale reddish-brown spots and streaks.
Clutch 3-5.

Food
Cone seeds, insects in summer; winter diet includes
seeds from birch and alder. Attracted to orange-
coloured 'Netlon' nut feeders in winter, when its
indifference to man is noticeable.

Goldfinch
Carduelis carduelis

Goldfinch

Size and Field Characteristics   12 cm.
Smaller than Chaffinch. A most attractive little bird.
Red, white and black head, fawn back, light under-parts,
black wings have striking golden-yellow wing bar, black
and white tail, sharp pointed beak. Sexes similar in
colouring.
Status
Resident.
Habitat and Range
Farmland, wasteland, orchards and gardens throughout
the British Isles, except for northern half of Scotland.
Nest
Built on outer branches of tree or hawthorn bush,
fashioned with moss, lichens, feathers and wool.
Eggs
Pale bluish spotted and streaked with brown. Clutch 5-6.
Food
Insects and weed seeds, especially thistle which the
Goldfinch extracts with its specialized beak, while
swinging pendulum-fashion on thistle heads.

Redpoll
Carduelis flammea

Redpoll

Size and Field Characteristics   ll.5 cm.
Size of Blue Tit. Light and dark brown streaked upper-parts, paler under-parts. Male has reddish forehead and breast, and black bib, female has black bib but forehead is less bright. Active and lively little birds, often seen in company of Siskins in topmost branches of alders and birch.
Status
Resident, some northern birds moving south for winter.
Habitat and Range
Scrubland, young conifer plantations, alder and birch woods, throughout most of British Isles.
Nest
Built in gorse or broom, young conifer or willow. A neat little cup of twigs and grasses, lined with white wild cotton down.
Eggs
Blue, spotted and streaked with brown. Clutch 4-6.
Food
Mainly birch and alder seeds, some insects.

Linnet
Carduelis cannabina

Linnet

Size and Field Characteristics 13 cm.
Smaller than Chaffinch. Male has chestnut brown back, greyish head, reddish forehead and breast, pale under-parts. Female lacks red, greyish head; brown streaked upper-parts. May be seen in flocks in autumn and winter.

Status
Resident.

Habitat and Range
Farmland, hedgerows, gorse covered scrub, young conifer plantations, large gardens and parks. Widespread throughout British Isles except for north-west Scotland.

Nest
In gorse or other protective bush, young conifer; built with grasses and moss, lined with hair and wool.

Eggs
Bluish-white, with purplish-red spots and streaks. Clutch 4-6.

Food
Mainly weed seeds, some insects.

Related Species
The Twite (*Carduelis flavirostris*) or 'Mountain Linnet' is a brown streaked little bird which breeds in north-west Scotland and the Pennines. Lacking in distinctive features, resembling female Linnet, yellow beak is best identification feature in winter when small flocks may be found in scrubby coastal areas.

Hawfinch
Coccothraustes coccothraustes

Hawfinch

Size and Field Characteristics 18 cm.
Larger than Chaffinch. Largest and shyest British
breeding Finch. Chestnut head, back and rump, pinkish
under-parts, black wings with white patches, black and
white tail. Large head and massive beak, good
identification feature.

Status
Resident.

Habitat and Range
Woodlands and orchards of the southern half of England
and south-west Scotland.

Nest
At times in small colonies, others singly in tree fork, built
with twigs, roots, moss and grasses.

Eggs
Creamy, with brownish markings and streaks. Clutch 4-6.

Food
Seeds and insects, the powerful beak capable of
breaking hard seeds and cherry stones. In summer the
Hawfinch prefers to feed among the tree tops. In winter
it will feed on wind-fall fruit on the ground.

Bullfinch
Pyrrhula pyrrhula

Bullfinch

Size and Field Characteristics 15 cm.
Similar in size to the Chaffinch, Bullfinches have black caps, white rumps and stubby bills. The male has a crimson breast while the female's is buffish-grey.
Status
Resident.
Habitat and Range
Woodland with patches of dense undergrowth, orchards, gardens and thick hedgerows. Widespread throughout the British Isles except for the far north.
Nest
A shallow cup built with fir twigs, lined with fine roots and hair. Seldom more than two metres from the ground.
Eggs
Pale green with purplish-brown spots and markings, mainly at the blunt end. Clutch 4-6.
Food
Kernels from seeds, buds, fruit and berries.

Crossbill
Loxia curvirostra

Crossbill

Size and Field Characteristics 16 cm.
Larger than Chaffinch. Large head with distinctly crossed
mandibles on bill. Male has brick-red plumage, brown
wings and tail. Female is yellowish-green with brown
wings and tail. Often seen at edge of conifer plantations,
where birds pick grit from road surface and bathe in and
drink from rain puddles and ditches.

Status
Resident and autumn migrant.

Habitat and Range
Conifer forests in south of England, Wales and Scotland.
In autumn 'irruptions' may occur when resident birds are
joined by large numbers from northern Europe. The
Scottish race (*Loxia scotica*) is confined to the old
Caledonian pine forests of northern Scotland.

Nest
Situated high in conifer, built with twigs, moss, grasses
and leaves, lined with fur and hair.

Eggs
Greenish-white, spotted and streaked with chestnut.
Clutch 3-4.

Food
The Crossbill's powerful jaw muscles, curious bill and
sticky tongue are ideal for extracting seeds from larch
and spruce cones, its staple diet. The Scottish Crossbill,
having a slightly larger, more powerful bill, is capable of
dealing with harder pine cones.

House Sparrow
Passer domesticus

House Sparrow

Size and Field Characteristics   14.5 cm.
Smaller than Chaffinch. A familiar bird in town and
country, often feeds from hand in town parks. Male has
brown and black streaked upper-parts, grey crown,
black throat, whitish cheeks and under-parts. Female is
duller, lacking the distinct head markings. 'City' House
Sparrows often have grimy-grey plumage, lacking the
lustre of their 'country' cousins.

Status
Resident.

Habitat and Range
In close association with man in town and country,
throughout the British Isles.

Nest
Two distinct types
(1) A bulky, domed construction of straw, grass and
feathers situated in hawthorn or other thick bush.
(2) Using same materials but built in a hole in building
or a crevice in monument, lamp standard etc.

Eggs
Greyish, finely speckled with blackish-brown. Clutch 4-6.

Food
Insects, seeds, grain, kitchen scraps. A regular visitor to
the bird table.

Tree Sparrow
Passer montanus

Tree Sparrow

Size and Field Characteristics 14 cm.
Smaller and more dapper than House Sparrow. Brown
and black streaked upper-parts, chocolate-brown crown,
white cheeks with black spot, black bib and pale under-
parts. Sexes similar in colouring. Much less associated
with man than House Sparrow. Roams with Finches and
Buntings in winter.
Status
Resident.
Habitat and Range
Open woodland and farmland throughout most of
England and Wales and the southern half of Scotland.
Nest
Usually in tree hole or nest-box, built with grasses, moss
and feathers.
Eggs
Whitish, densely speckled with brown. Clutch 4-6.
Food
Mainly seeds, grain and insects.

Starling
Sturnus vulgaris

Starling

Size and Field Characteristics   21.5 cm.
Smaller than Blackbird. A very clever mimic, able to
imitate human whistles as well as other bird sounds. A
short-tailed black-plumaged bird, spotted in appearance
in winter, less so in breeding season. Starlings are active
and sprightly. Starlings present an exciting spectacle
when many thousands gather together in sky above
winter roost.
Status
Resident.
Habitat and Range
From open country to city centres throughout the British
Isles.
Nest
In tree hole, hole in building (usually on wall head
under slates), various other cavities large enough to
accept the twig, grass and feather construction.
Eggs
Pale blue. Clutch 4-6.
Food
Insects, grubs, earthworms, fruit, berries, kitchen scraps.

Waxwing
Bombycilla garrulus

Waxwing

Size and Field Characteristics 18 cm.
Smaller than Starling. Exotic appearance. Plumage is buffish brown, pink and grey with black chin and throat. Rich chestnut erectile crest, yellow tip to short dark tail. Dark wings with white and yellow markings, also have waxy red tips to some feathers, hence the name Waxwing. Can appear singly or in flock of up to around fifty, and may be approached quite close without birds showing signs of alarm.

Status
Winter visitor.

Habitat and Range
Rural or urban, wherever food is available. Visitors mainly to east coast of Britain but during 'irruptions', when overcrowding or food shortage occurs in northern Europe, may be seen further inland.

Food
While visiting British Isles food consists almost entirely of red berries, such as rowan, hawthorn, cotoneaster and wild rose.

Dunnock
Prunella modularis

Dunnock

Size and Field Characteristics 14.5 cm.
Slightly smaller than Chaffinch. Sometimes called Hedge
Sparrow, but thin bill differs from Sparrow species.
Upper-parts, wings and tail streaked with shades of
brown and black, head, neck and breast slate-grey, pale
grey under-parts. Skulks around hedge or bush bottoms.
Status
Resident
Habitat and Range
Woodland, copses, roadside hedgerows, farmland and
gardens provide breeding habitat for Dunnocks.
Widespread throughout British Isles.
Nest
Built in hedge, low bush or low in conifer and
constructed with twigs, leaves, moss, hair and feathers.
Eggs
Deep blue. Clutch 4-5.
Food
Mainly weed seeds and insects. In winter, when seen in
garden, tends to feed under rather than on bird table.

Robin
Erithacus rubecula

Robin

Size and Field Characteristics 14 cm.
Slightly shorter than Chaffinch. A most familiar small bird. Brown upper-parts, distinctive orange-red face and breast, whitish belly and pale under-parts. Friendly towards man during winter, secretive during breeding season.

Status
Resident.

Habitat and Range
Prefers open woodland and large gardens as breeding haunts. In winter moves closer to human habitation. Widespread throughout British Isles

Nest
Built in a hollow in a wide variety of places, including banks and tree roots, and many sites in sheds and outbuildings.

Eggs
White, spotted with reddish-orange. Clutch 4-5.

Food
Insects, worms, caterpillars, seeds and table scraps, which Robin will on occasion enter house to obtain.

Nightingale
Luscinia megarbynchos

Nightingale

Size and Field Characteristics   16.5 cm.
Larger than Chaffinch. Upper-parts plain brown, chestnut tail and pale grey under-parts. Shy and secretive but, when seen in open, stance is upright like that of Robin. Distinctive song, heard during the day as well as at night, best identification feature.

Status
Summer resident.

Habitat and Range
Woodlands and coppices with patches of thick, tangled undergrowth. Breeds in south-east England; winters in Africa south of the Sahara.

Nest
Built among brambles or other dense vegetation, close to the ground, constructed with leaves and grasses and lined with finer grass and hair.

Eggs
Bluish-green to olive. Clutch 4-6.

Food
Rummages for insects on the ground, also eats seeds, berries and soft fruit.

Redstart
Phoenicurus phoenicurus

Redstart

Size and Field Characteristics 14 cm.
Size of Robin. Male has greyish crown and mantle,
white forehead and black face; rump, under-parts and
tail are rusty-red, hence the name Redstart. Female is
dull brown with reddish tail. Tail is frequently twitched,
good identification feature in poor light.

Status
Summer resident.

Habitat and Range
Prefers open deciduous woodland with dead or dying
trees with holes for nesting, also parkland and gardens.
Found throughout most of British Isles. Winters in Sahel
Zone, south of Sahara Desert in Africa.

Nest
In tree hole, hole in wall, nest-box. Built with moss,
fibres, feathers and hair.

Eggs
Pale blue. Clutch 5-7.

Food
Insects, taken both in the air and from the ground
among short vegetation.

Black Redstart
Phoenicurus ochruros

Black Redstart

Size and Field Characteristics   14 cm.
Size of Robin. Male has black upper-parts and breast
with paler patches on wings; rump and tail rusty-red.
Female has greyish-brown body with rusty-red tail.
Perches prominently on rock or wall.

Status
Resident and passage migrant.

Habitat and Range
Derelict buildings, large railway yards with sheds and
piles of rubble, old harbourside warehouses. Breeds in
south-east England, moves to coastal regions in winter.

Nest
In hole in wall or crevice in sea cliff; built with grasses
and lined with feathers.

Eggs
White. Clutch 4-6.

Food
Almost entirely insects and spiders.

Long-Tailed Tit
Aegithalos caudatus

Long-Tailed Tit

Size and Field Characteristics 14 cm, including 8 cm long tail, making it longer than Chaffinch.
A distance relative of the Tit family. Black mantle and wings and tail with white outer tail feathers, white crown, face and under-parts, broad black eye-stripe, pinkish shoulders and undertail. Often encountered in roving flocks during winter when they can be observed from close proximity.

Status
Resident.

Habitat and Range
Broad-leaved woodland, scrub, hedgerows and large gardens. Throughout the British Isles.

Nest
Unlike other members of the Tit family does not nest in a hole, but builds a compact, domed structure with moss, hair and spiders webs, covered with lichen and copiously lined with feathers, situated about two metres from ground in gorse, blackthorn, conifer or thick bush.

Eggs
White, faintly spotted with reddish-brown. Clutch 8-12.

Food
Mainly insects or spiders in summer; in winter, occasionally visits bird tables, a trend which is on the increase.

Willow Tit
Parus montanus

Willow Tit

Size and Field Characteristics   ll.5 cm.
Similar size to Blue Tit. Greyish-brown back and wings,
pale under-parts, white face, black cap, nape and bib.
Status
Resident.
Habitat and Range
Deciduous woodland with damp boggy patches and old
decaying trees. Widespread throughout England, Wales
and southern Scotland.
Nest
A hole excavated by the pair in a soft rotten tree stump,
lined with wood chips, fine grasses and rabbit fur.
Eggs
White, spotted with reddish-brown. Clutch 6-8.
Food
Insects, caterpillars, spiders, some seeds and berries.
Related Species
The Marsh Tit (*Parus palustris*) is similar in size and
colouring to Willow Tit, but has glossy sheen to black
head. Best identification feature is 'pitchu-pitchu' call of
Marsh Tit compared to 'tsi-tsi-tsi' call of Willow Tit. Both
species have similar British range. Marsh Tits do not
excavate nest holes like Willow Tit, but usually nest in a
tree hole.

Blue Tit
Parus caeruleus

Blue Tit

Size and Field Characteristics ll.5 cm.
A most familiar, active and colourful little bird, easily recognised when it visits bird-tables. Yellowish-green back, blue cap, wings and tail, white face with black eye-stripe, yellow underside.

Status
Resident.

Habitat and Range
Woodland, parkland and gardens throughout British Isles.

Nest
In hole in tree, wall or other convenient cavity. Readily uses nest-boxes. Nest built with moss, hair and feathers.

Eggs
White with faint reddish spots. Clutch 7-12.

Food
Insects and caterpillars in summer. Constant visitor to nut-feeders and bird tables in winter.

Great Tit
Parus major

Great Tit

Size and Field Characteristics   14 cm.
Slightly smaller than Chaffinch. Easily identified by
largish size, black head with conspicuous white cheeks
and black band running from chin down centre of
yellow breast to undertail.
Status
Resident.
Habitat and Range
Woodland, parkland and gardens throughout the British
Isles.
Nest
In tree hole, hollow gate post, upturned plant pot, nest-
box. Built with moss, hair and feathers.
Eggs
White with reddish spots. Clutch 7-12.
Food
Insects, caterpillars, buds. Constant visitor to nut-feeders
and bird tables in winter.

Crested Tit
Parus cristatus

Crested Tit

Size and Field Characteristics   ll.5 cm.
Similar size to Blue Tit. Black and white crest, only small British bird to possess such adornment. Brown back and tail, pale under-parts, white face, black chin and collar, black ear-shaped mark from eye to lower cheek. Often difficult to identify from below as birds frequent pine canopies. Best identification feature is distinctive trilling call.

Status
Resident.

Habitat and Range
The old pine forests of northern Scotland.

Nest
Usually hole excavated in decaying pine tree stump, lined with moss, hair and wool.

Eggs
White blotched with reddish markings. Clutch 5-6.

Food
Insects, caterpillars, fruit and seeds.

Coal Tit
Parus ater

Coal Tit

Size and Field Characteristics   11 cm.
Slightly smaller than Blue Tit, smallest British Tit.
Greenish-grey back, tail and wings, wings have two
white bars; pale underparts. Black crown and bib, white
cheeks and white triangular patch on back of head.
Status
Resident
Habitat and Range
Woodlands, especially conifer, throughout the British
Isles.
Nest
In holes in walls, tree bottoms or bankings. Ground
next-boxes covered with thin layer of soil in conifer
forests often accepted. Nest built with moss, hair and
feathers.
Eggs
White with pale reddish-brown spots. Clutch 6-12.
Food
Seeds and insects for which the Coal Tit's slender bill is
ideal. Coal Tits also visit bird tables in winter, to a lesser
degree that Blue or Great Tits, taking small morsels to
hide away.

Nuthatch
Sitta europaea

Nuthatch

Size and Field Characteristics   14 cm.
Slightly smaller than Chaffinch. An active bird which
can climb down tree trunks as easily as it climbs up.
Large head, longish stout bill, short tail. Bluish-grey
head, back and tail, prominent black eye-stripe,
contrasting white chin and cheeks, pale orange-buff
under-parts.
Status
Resident.
Habitat and Range
Woodland parkland and gardens throughout most of
England and Wales, rare in Scotland.
Nest
Usually in a tree hole, where the Nuthatches reduce the
entrance size by 'plastering' round the rim with mud.
Nest-boxes receive the same precautionary measure to
deter other hole nesters. Pieces of bark and leaves
deposited on floor of hole in untidy fashion.
Eggs
White with reddish-brown spots. Clutch 6-l0.
Food
Insects, acorns and various nuts, the Nuthatch being
capable of cracking open hazelnuts and walnuts.

Jay
Garrulus glandarius

Jay

Size and Field Characteristics   34 cm.
Smaller than Wood Pigeon. Most colourful member of
Crow family. Shy and flighty. Pinkish-brown body;
prominent white rump contrasts with black tail; black,
white and blue wings. Black and white streaked erectile
crown feathers. Black 'moustache' and stout bill.

Status
Resident.

Habitat and Range
Deciduous and conifer woods, parkland, farmland and
gardens. Widespread throughout England and Wales,
confined to south and central belt in Scotland.

Nest
Built in conifer or thick bush with twigs, rootlets and
grasses; cup-shaped.

Eggs
Greenish, speckled with faint brown markings and a few
black hair lines. Clutch 3-6.

Food
Insects, young birds and eggs, seeds and fruit. In
autumn, collects and stores acorns – many oaks have
been planted in this way. Also visits bird tables.

Tree Creeper
Certhia familiaris

Tree Creeper

Size and Field Characteristics 12.5 cm.
Smaller than Chaffinch. Mouse-like as it climbs upwards
in spiralling fashion from base of tree trunk. Brown and
buff streaked upper-parts, pale eye-stripe, white under-
parts, long toes, stiff tail, longish, slender down-curved
bill.

Status
Resident.

Habitat and Range
Woodland and parkland with decaying and dead trees
throughout most of British Isles.

Nest
In tree crevice or behind loose bark, occasionally in
nest-box. Built with twigs and stalks and lined with
feathers.

Eggs
White with reddish brown speckles. Clutch 5-6.

Food
Insects and larvae, spiders and their eggs, for which the
Tree Creeper probes into tree cracks using its specialized
bill.

Magpie
Pica pica

Magpie

Size and Field Characteristics   46 cm including 22 cm long tail.

Larger than Jackdaw. Glossy black head, mantle and breast; white under-parts and wing patches. Wing tips and long tail glossy green with purplish highlights. On the ground the tail is held in elevated position.

Status

Resident.

Habitat and Range

Scrubland by woodland edge, farmland, urban gardens and parks throughout England and Wales, patchy distribution in Scotland.

Nest

Cup-shaped structure made with grasses, roots, fibres and mud, covered by protective dome of hawthorn twigs. Usually sited in hawthorn bush or tall tree.

Eggs

Bluish-green speckled with brownish-grey. Clutch 4-7.

Food

Invertebrates, grain, seeds, fruit, eggs, chicks, carrion and kitchen scraps.

Jackdaw
Corvus monedula

Jackdaw

Size and Field Characteristics 33 cm.
Smaller than Rook. Black plumage, black legs and beak, back of head grey. Gregarious at all times, often seen feeding in fields with Rooks.
Status
Resident.
Habitat and Range
Equally at home in town or country throughout British Isles except for far north-west Scotland.
Nest
Built in tree hole, rabbit burrow, chimney or church tower, where the nest may be extremely bulky, a mass of twigs, paper, hair and wool.
Eggs
Pale blue, spotted with dark-grey. Clutch 3-5.
Food
Insects, invertebrates, seeds, grain, berries and kitchen scraps.

Rook
Corvus frugilegus

Rook

Size and Field Characteristics 46 cm.
Larger than Wood Pigeon. A large black bird with 'baggy pants' and bare grey skin patch at base of the beak. Rooks are gregarious at all times.
Status
Resident.
Habitat and Range
Farmland and woodland throughout the British Isles except for patches of north and west Scotland.
Nest
Built colonially in rookery, bulky structures of sticks, twigs, leaves, grasses and wool. Rookeries may be located in both deciduous and conifer woods.
Eggs
Greyish-green with ash-grey markings. Clutch 3-5.
Food
Earthworms, grubs, insects and grain.

Wood Pigeon
Columba palumbus

Wood Pigeon

Size and Field Characteristics 40 cm.
Largest native Dove. Bluish-grey head and back, darker
wingtips and tip of tail, pinkish tinge to breast, white
patches on side of neck, and white wing bars
conspicuous in flight. Distinct 'co-cooo-coo, coo, coo'
call.
Status
Resident, numbers increased in winter.
Habitat and Range
Woodland, farmland, town and city parks. Widespread
throughout most of British Isles, with numbers increased
in winter by Scandinavian birds.
Nest
A platform of sticks and twigs, at times flimsy, at others
quite bulky – from very low, occasionally on ground, to
several metres above ground in tall trees.
Eggs
White. Clutch 2.
Food
Grain, cereals, vegetable shoots, acorns.

Stock Dove
Columba oenas

Stock Dove

Size and Field Characteristics   32 cm.
Smaller than Wood Pigeon. Greyish-blue head and back
with darker wing tips and tip of tail, also two small dark
wing bars. Fluorescent-green patches on sides of neck,
grey rump, pinkish tinge to breast.

Status
Resident.

Habitat and Range
Old woodland, farmland and fields. Widespread
throughout England and Wales. Scarce above central belt
of Scotland.

Nest
Platform of twigs in tree hole, bushy growth on side of
tree, large nest-box or ledge in derelict farm building.

Eggs
White. Clutch 2.

Food
Seeds, grain, young plants.

Related Species
The Rock Dove (*Columba livia*) is similar in size to the
Stock Dove, slightly greyer in colour, with two distinct
black wing bars and a noticeable white rump. The Rock
Dove is the ancestor of today's racing Pigeons. Colonies
of true Rock Doves can be found on the north-west coast
of Scotland, with smaller family groups in some remote
inland rocky wooded glens.

Collared Dove
Streptopelia decaocto

Collared Dove

Size and Field Characteristics 32 cm.
Smaller than Wood Pigeon. Pinkish-white breast and
head with distinct black half collar, pale brownish-grey
wings with darker tips, longish tail has white outer
feathers, short reddish legs and short black beak.

Status
Resident.

Habitat and Range
Farmland, suburban gardens and parks with evergreens.
Widespread throughout the British Isles.

Nest
Flimsy, twiggy platform, in dark-foliaged tree, close to
the trunk.

Eggs
White. Clutch 2.

Food
Grain, seeds, shoots of young garden plants, making it a
nuisance to the gardener.

Turtle Dove
Streptopelia turtur

Turtle Dove

Size and Field Characteristics 32 cm.
Smaller than Wood Pigeon. Chestnut-brown and dark
grey patterned back with darker wing tips, pale head
breast and under-parts with pinkish tinge, black and
white patches on neck, white tips to other feathers of
long tail, short reddish legs and short black beak.
Status
Summer resident, the only British Dove in this category.
Habitat and Range
Low-lying farmland, woodland edges and overgrown
hedgerows. Widespread throughout most of England
except for the north and the eastern half of Wales,
occasionally seen in Scotland. Winters in Africa, south
of the Sahara.
Nest
Twiggy platforms in high hedge or tree, away from
human habitation.
Eggs
White. Clutch 2.
Food
Grain, weed seeds, plant shoots and buds.

Garden Warbler
Sylvia borin

Garden Warbler

Size and Field Characteristics 14 cm.
Slightly smaller than Chaffinch. Plainest of Warblers,
pale brown back, light under-parts, with no obvious
distinguishing marks, sexes similar in colour. Melodious
song is best identification feature in territory.
Status
Summer resident.
Habitat and Range
Open woodland with dense undergrowth. Widespread
throughout England, Wales and southern half of
Scotland. Winters in Africa.
Nest
A grassy cup, lined with finer fibres, built in
undergrowth, about one metre from ground. Female
selects one of several cocks' nests built by her mate.
Eggs
Pale greyish colour, with brown and grey markings.
Clutch 4-6.
Food
Mainly insects.

Blackcap
Sylvia atricapilla

Blackcap

Size and Field Characteristics 14 cm.
Slightly smaller than Chaffinch. Male has greyish back
and tail, with paler under-parts, and distinct black cap.
Female has similar plumage but with brown cap.
Status
Mainly summer resident, with some birds from north-east
Europe wintering in Britain.
Habitat and Range
In summer, open woodlands with dense undergrowth, in
winter, parklands and gardens. British breeding birds
winter in Africa.
Nest
A grassy cup lined with finer fibres, built among wild
raspberry canes or other herbage, about one metre from
ground.
Eggs
Pale greyish colour, flecked with brown and grey
markings. Clutch 4-5.
Food
In summer, mainly insects. In winter, berries; also visits
garden bird-tables, where it is seen to be aggressive
toward other species.

Willow Warbler
Phylloscopus trochilus

Willow Warbler

Size and Field Characteristics ll cm.
Smaller than Blue Tit. Most common of the three
'Greenish' or 'Leaf' Warblers. Adult plumage ranges
from pale brown to olive-brown upper-parts, white to
buffish under-parts, yellowish breast and paler eye-
stripe. Best distinguished from Chiffchaff by its song, a
series of notes trickling down the scale.

Status
Summer resident.

Habitat and Range
Woodland, scrub and large gardens. Widespread
throughout Britain. Winters in east Africa.

Nest
Well concealed in grassy tussock or at times in lower
branches of conifer about one metre from ground. A
domed structure, built with moss, grass and leaves and
lined with feathers.

Eggs
White, finely spotted with pale reddish-brown.
Clutch 6-7.

Food
Mainly insects and caterpillars.

Chiffchaff
Phylloscopus collybita

Chiffchaff

Size and Field Characteristics ll cm.
Smaller than Blue Tit. One of the three 'Greenish' or
'Leaf' Warblers. Plumage is identical to Willow Warbler,
brownish-olive upper-parts, whitish under-parts,
yellowish breast and pale eye-stripe. Chiffchaff may be
seen to have darker legs. Surest identification feature is
'chip-chap' 'chip-chip-chap' song, entirely different from
that of Willow Warbler.

Status
Summer resident.

Habitat and Range
Woodland and scrub, throughout British Isles except for
most of the northern half of Scotland. Except for a few
that linger in the south of England, Chiffchaffs winter
around the Mediterranean.

Nest
A domed structure, built with grass and leaves and lined
with hair and feathers. Usually situated low in
undergrowth.

Eggs
White with dark reddish-brown spots. Clutch 5-6.

Food
Mainly insects and caterpillars taken from tree canopy at
higher level than feeding Willow Warblers.

Wood Warbler
Phylloscopus sibilatrix

Wood Warbler

Size and Field Characteristics   13 cm.
Smaller than Chaffinch. The largest of the three
'Greenish' or 'Leaf' Warblers. Yellowish-green upper-
parts, bright yellow throat and breast with white belly
and yellow eye-stripe. Song differs from both Willow
Warbler and Chiffchaff, being more melodious, 'tsu-tsu-
tsu' ending with a trill.

Status
Summer resident.

Habitat and Range
Mature oak and beech woodland, preferably with
sloping ground and clear patches. Widespread
throughout Britain, but scarce in parts of north and east.
Winters in Africa.

Nest
A domed structure, built with dead leaves and grass,
lined with hair, and well concealed on ground.

Eggs
White, spotted with violet-brown. Clutch 5-7.

Food
Mainly insects, spiders and caterpillars, taken from
foliage high in tree canopy.

Goldcrest
Regulus regulus

Goldcrest

Size and Field Characteristics   9 cm.
Smallest British bird. Olive-green upper-parts with darker
tail and wings, wings have two whitish bars, pale under-
parts. Male has orange, yellow and black crown,
female's is yellow and black. Goldcrests are active little
birds with large eyes and thin pointed insectivorous bills.

Status
Resident, numbers increased by Scandinavian birds in
winter.

Habitat and Range
Woodland especially coniferous. Widespread throughout
British Isles.

Nest
Deep hammock-styled cup, attached to underside of
coniferous branch by mossy strands and cobwebs, built
with mosses, cobwebs, hair and feathers.

Eggs
Pinkish-white with faint spots. Clutch 7-l0.

Food
Insects, their eggs and larvae.

Related Species
The equally tiny Firecrest (*Regulus ignicapillus*) is mainly
a rare spring and autumn migrant. Small scattered
colonies of breeding birds occur in England and Wales.
Firecrests are equally at home in broad-leaved or conifer
woods.

Spotted Flycatcher
Muscicapa striata

Spotted Flycatcher

Size and Field Characteristics 14 cm.
Smaller than Chaffinch. A sleek, drab-coloured little
bird, with upright stance. Greyish-brown upper-parts
with dark streaks on flattish head, under-parts whitish
with a few darker streaks on breast.
Status
Summer resident.
Habitat and Range
Open woodland, parkland and gardens throughout
Britain. One of our latest summer residents to arrive
from Africa, returning after a brief visit of about twelve
weeks.
Nest
Built in hollow in wall, tree, pipe or in open-fronted
nest-box, a cup-shaped structure of twigs, roots, leaves
and hair.
Eggs
Greyish with reddish-brown flecks. Clutch 4-5.
Food
Flying insects. The Spotted Flycatcher is best identified
while feeding. From a prominent perch it darts forward,
and following a few erratic twists and turns, returns to
point of departure or close to it, this procedure is
repeated several times.

Pied Flycatcher
Ficedula bypoleuca

Pied Flycatcher

Size and Field Characteristics   13 cm.
Smaller than Chaffinch. Male in spring has black upper-parts with white forehead and wing patches, pure white under-parts. In autumn, plumage resembles that of browner female.

Status
Summer resident.

Habitat and Range
Open, broad-leaved woodland, particularly upland valleys. Seen as a migrant throughout most of Britain. Breeding restricted to areas where habitat is suitable, the wooded hillsides of Wales, northern England, south and eastern Scotland. Winters in Africa.

Nest
Usually hole in tree, built with birchbark, grass, leaves and hair. Woodland populations greatly increased by erection of nest-boxes, which are readily accepted.

Eggs
Pale glossy blue. Clutch 5-8.

Food
Flying insects, also insects and caterpillars picked from leaves, branches and ground.

Wren
Troglodytes troglodytes

Wren

Size and Field Characteristics 9.5 cm.
A dumpy little bird with stumpy cocked tail. Reddish brown upper-parts with darker barring on wings and tail, paler under-parts and eye-stripe, thin bill. Strident, warbling song for such a tiny bird, good identification feature. In winter, communal roosts such as nest-boxes may be found to contain in excess of forty birds

Status
Resident.

Habitat and Range
Found almost everywhere in British Isles, from low-lying woodland and gardens to high moorland and rocky burns.

Nest
Male Wren builds several nests, using twigs, leaves and moss, concealed under upturned tree root, in bushy growth, young conifer or outbuilding, female selects one, lines it with feathers and commences laying.

Eggs
White with reddish-brown spots. Clutch 4-8.

Food
Mainly insects and caterpillars.

Swift
Apus apus

Swift

Size and Field Characteristics l7 cm, wing span 33 cm.
Often mistaken for a member of the Swallow family.
Smaller body than Starling but longer wing span. Dark
brown plumage with pale throat. Scythe-shaped wings
and short forked tail, short legs with all four toes pointing
forward. Totally aerial, eats, sleeps, drinks, gathers nesting
material and mates in the air. Parties of screaming birds
skimming over roof-tops easily identified.

Status
Summer resident.

Habitat and Range
From May to July Swifts can be seen in the sky,
throughout the whole of Britain except for the extreme
north-west of Scotland. Winters in Africa.

Nest
In a hole under the eaves of buildings, usually adding
slight feather lining to old Starling nest on top of wall
head.

Eggs
White. Clutch 2-3.
Eggs have staggered hatching, thus ensuring that at least
one youngster will survive a prolonged cold or wet spell.

Food
Entirely flying insects caught in wide gape, young fed on
ball of insects trapped in parent's throat as it sweeps
continually through the air.

Green Woodpecker
Picus viridis

Green Woodpecker

Size and Field Characteristics 32 cm.
Slightly smaller than Jackdaw. Largest British
Woodpecker. Dark green back, yellowish rump,
greyish-green striped wing tips and tail, pale yellow
under-parts, red crown, black cheeks, male has red
moustachial stripe, strong, chisel-like bill about same
length as head. Green Woodpeckers fly in an
undulating manner.

Status
Resident.

Habitat and Range
Mature woodland and parkland with trees. Widespread
throughout England and Wales. Patchy in Scotland,
established in the south and around central belt.

Nest
In tree such an an alder from three to fifteen metres
above the ground, a hole chipped in, then downward to
form a chamber. The eggs are laid on the loose
chippings on the floor of the chamber.

Eggs
White. Clutch 5-8.

Food
Grubs of wood-boring insects, which are located by
tapping decaying wood with bill. Also feeds on ants,
extracting the ants and their pupae with a long sticky
tongue.

Great Spotted Woodpecker
Dendrocopus major

Great Spotted Woodpecker

Size and Field Characteristics   23 cm.
Smaller than Blackbird. Black and white head, back,
wings and tail, with white shoulder patches conspicuous
in flight. Male has red patch on nape, both sexes have
bright red undertail. Sharp pointed bill slightly less than
length of head. Undulating flight, like that of other
Woodpeckers. In early spring the Great Spotted
Woodpeckers' drumming sound can be heard as the
birds rap on dead branches, during their territorial
display.
Status
Resident.
Habitat and Range
Favours mature mixed woodland, with dead and
decaying trees, large gardens, and wild hedgerows with
trees. Widespread throughout the woodlands of England,
Wales and Scotland.
Nest
Hole and chamber in dead or decaying tree which is
excavated by the Woodpeckers, in and then downward.
The height of the nest hole from the ground can vary
from two metres to over twelve metres.
Eggs
White. Clutch 5-6.
Food
Wood-boring insects and their larvae, seeds, nuts and
berries.

Lesser Spotted Woodpecker
Dendrocopus minor

Lesser Spotted Woodpecker

Size and Field Characteristics 14 cm.
Slightly smaller than Chaffinch. Black and white barred
back and wings, white under-parts slightly streaked with
black. Male has red crown, female's is whitish. Stiff tail
feathers like other Woodpeckers and similar undulating
flight. Spends most of its time in high tree tops.

Status
Resident.

Habitat and Range
Deciduous woodland, large gardens and orchards and
parklands. Found throughout most of England and
Wales.

Nest
Hole and chamber in soft, rotting wood usually on
underside of branch one to fifteen metres above ground.
No material used to line chamber.

Eggs
White. Clutch 3-7.

Food
Insects and their larvae.

Related Species
The Wryneck (*Jynx torquilla*), 15 cm, is a close relative of
the Woodpeckers, appearing in the British Isles as a rare
summer resident and passage migrant. The plumage is
greyish brown, streaked with dark brown, under-parts
paler and slightly barred. Unique habit of twisting its
head round, hence its name. Rare breeder in old Scottish
pine woods. Passage migrant to east coast of England.

Swallow
Hirundo rustica

Swallow

Size and Field Characteristics   19 cm, including long
tail 'streamers'.
Bluish-black upper-parts; white under-parts; dark red
face and long, brown outer tail feathers, by which the
Swallow is easily recognised in flight or at rest on
telephone wires etc. Seen collectively on telegraph
wires prior to autumn departure.

Status
Summer resident.

Habitat and Range
Closely associated with farm buildings; rural and
suburban habitat. Widespread throughout the British
Isles. Winters in Africa.

Nest
A saucer-shaped construction of mud, straw and
feathers, built on a beam or other suitable ledge in open
farm building, shed or outhouse.

Eggs
White with purplish-brown spots. Clutch 4-6.

Food
Flying insects which the Swallow catches in its wide
gape as it skims low over pastures, ponds and rivers.

House Martin
Delichon urbica

House Martin

Size and Field Characteristics 12.5 cm.
Smaller than Swallow. Dark blue upper-parts; white
under-parts and rump, forked tail, feet feathered to toes.
Like Swallow, seen collectively on telegraph wires prior
to autumn departure.

Status
Summer resident.

Habitat and Range
Human habitation of both town and country, throughout
the British Isles except for extreme north of Scotland.
Winters in Africa.

Nest
A clever construction of mud, saliva and feathers with
entrance hole at top, built under eaves of houses or
ledges on bridges, usually colonial.

Eggs
White. Clutch 4-6.

Food
Flying insects, caught on the wing by the House Martin
sweeping to and fro through the air, usually at a higher
level than the feeding Swallows.

Woodlark
Lullula arborea

Woodlark

Size and Field Characteristics 15 cm.
Size of Chaffinch. Light and dark brown streaked upper-parts, pale under-parts with dark streaks on breast, chestnut cheeks, white eye-stripes which meet at back of head, short tail noticeable in flight, melodious song. More solitary than the Skylark in winter.
Status
Resident.
Habitat and Range
Dry heathland and downland with scattered trees, areas of recently planted or cleared timber. Distribution is patchy, confined to areas of southern and eastern England.
Nest
Well concealed among scrubby vegetation, a neat grass cup, lined with finer grasses.
Eggs
Pale greyish colour, mottled and spotted with shades of brown and grey. Clutch 3-4.
Food
Insects and small invertebrates, seeds.

Tree Pipit
Anthus trivialis

Tree Pipit

Size and Field Characteristics 15 cm.
Similar size to Chaffinch. Upper-parts olive-brown,
streaked with dark brown, under-parts paler but also
streaked and spotted with brown. Tree Pipit rises into
air from tree branch vantage point, bursts into song, then
parachutes down with wings and tail spread, often
returning to its point of departure. This behaviour good
identification feature.

Status
Summer resident.

Habitat and Range
Open woodland and edges of denser woods, are
favoured breeding haunts throughout most of the British
Isles. Winters in Africa.

Nest
Built with grasses, bents and moss, lined with fine
grasses and concealed in grassy tussock on ground or
bank.

Eggs
Variable, from reddish to grey, finely marked.
Clutch 4-6.

Food
Insects, spiders, seeds.

Barn Owl
Tyto alba

Barn Owl

Size and Field Characteristics   34 cm.
Smaller than Wood Pigeon. Nocturnal – active at night.
Upper-parts golden-brown flecked with grey, contrast
with snow-white under-parts and heart-shaped face.
Hooked beak and needle-sharp talons, the outer toe
being reversible, allowing more secure grip on prey.
Barn Owls do not hoot but utter a startling shriek.
Status
Resident.
Habitat and Range
Farmland, old woodland and open ground. Widespread
throughout England, Wales and the southern half of
Scotland, but becoming scarce in most places.
Nest
In derelict farm building, hay loft, large nest box or hole
in tree; no material added but eggs sometimes laid on
bed of crumbled 'pellets' in traditional site.
Eggs
White. Clutch 4-10.
Food
Mainly small mammals, occasionally small birds. 'Pellets'
are round or sausage-shaped castings 4-7 cm in length,
which consist of the indigestible parts of the Owl's diet.
The regurgitated pellet of bones, fur etc. is ejected from
the beak.

Little Owl
Athene noctua

Little Owl

Size and Field Characteristics 22 cm.
Size of Starling, with typical Owl shape. White-spotted, brown upper-parts, brown streaked under-parts, flattish-topped head and yellow eyes. Often seen perched on post or tree limb during daylight hours (good identification feature) but prefers to search for prey at dusk.

Status
Resident.

Habitat and Range
Farmland with rough field edges and scattered trees, waste and open ground, hedgerows. Widely distributed throughout England and Wales, but only a foothold in southern Scotland.

Nest
Usually in tree hole, hole in wall, nest-box or haystack, some sites used continuously for many years.

Eggs
White. Clutch 2-5.

Food
Small mammals, birds, beetles, insects and 'dew' worms.

Tawny Owl
Strix aluco

Tawny Owl

Size and Field Characteristics 38 cm.
Smaller than Wood Pigeon. The most common Owl in
Britain. Nocturnal, dozes daylight hours away in some
concealed nook. Plumage can be predominantly brown
or grey, both varieties covered in markings of grey, buff
and brown. Large black eyes, rounded wings and short
tail. Male utters familiar 'hoo, hoo, hoo-ooo' call in
territory, answered by female's short 'kewit'.

Status
Resident.

Habitat and Range
Woodlands, both broad-leaved and conifer, farmland
and parkland. Widespread throughout England, Wales
and Scotland.

Nest
Tree-hole, old crow or hawk nest, large nest-box, ledge
in derelict or open farm building

Eggs
White. Clutch 2-4.

Food
Small mammals, birds, beetles and earthworms.

Long-eared Owl
Asio otus

Long-eared Owl

Size and Field Characteristics 35 cm.
Slightly smaller than Tawny Owl. When seen perched,
its slimmer shape makes it seem larger. Upper-parts
buffish, mottled in brown and grey and streaked with
darker brown; under-parts also buffish streaked with
dark brown, orange eyes. Displays two noticeable 'ear'
tufts when alarmed, these are adornments, not ears.
Status
Resident.
Habitat and Range
Nocturnal through most of its breeding range in British
Isles, less so in extreme north of the country. Prefers
dense woodland in the south, may be seen on open
rough ground in north. Absent from most of the western
edge of the country.
Nest
Does not build nest, lays eggs in old nest of crow, hawk,
pigeon etc. or on ground among rough vegetation.
Eggs
White. Clutch 3-5.
Food
Small mammals, birds, beetles.

Buzzard
Buteo buteo

Buzzard

Size and Field Characteristics Male 54 cm, female 58 cm.
The Buzzard is a large bird of prey. Although Buzzards are predominantly dark-brown on the upper-parts with lighter, barred under-parts, some individuals are much paler. In flight they soar effortlessly, rising in the up-draught from the side of a hill or in a thermal. At rest they perch on trees and poles in a hunched position. Buzzards have much smaller beaks in comparison to the size of their heads than Golden Eagles.

Status
Resident.

Habitat and Range
Rolling hills with woodland and farmland over practically the whole of Scotland and Wales but scarce in most of England, especially in the east.

Nest
Usually in tree fork; bulky, built with sticks, branches, grass and wool.

Eggs
Off-white, variably marked with reddish-brown. Clutch 2-5.

Food
Rabbits, rodents, birds, insects and carrion.

Sparrowhawk
Accipiter nisus

Sparrowhawk

Size and Field Characteristics 28-38 cm.
Smaller than Pigeon. Male has slate-grey upper-parts,
orange-tinged, barred breast, and light and dark grey
barred long tail. The female is brownish grey on the
upper-parts with brown barred breast and long tail. The
female is noticeably larger than male.
Status
Resident.
Habitat and Range
Open woodland, forests, birch scrub, farmland and
hedgerows. Widespread throughout the British Isles but
scarce in south-east England.
Nest
A large flat structure built with sticks and twigs, most
often sited high in a conifer but also in other trees.
Eggs
Bluish-white, variably marked with reddish-brown.
Clutch 4-5.
Food
Practically entirely birds, from Wrens to Doves, which
are secured following a swift, dashing chase.

Goshawk
Accipiter gentilis

Goshawk

Size and Field Characteristics   50-60 cm.
Female almost Buzzard size, male noticeably smaller.
The male Goshawk is slightly larger than a female
Sparrow Hawk but of much stockier build. In flight, the
wings are more curved and the tail is noticeably shorter.
The female, like her mate, is brownish-grey on the
upper-parts, with fine grey and white barring on her
breast.
Status
Resident.
Habitat and Range
Conifer forests and woodlands throughout most of the
British Isles. Breeding range more restricted.
Nest
Usually high in conifer, a bulky construction of sticks,
branches, grass and dead leaves.
Eggs
Bluish-white. Clutch 2-5.
Food
Birds up to the size of Capercaillie, mammals up to the
size of hare.

Red Kite
Milvus milvus

Red Kite

Size and Field Characteristics 60-64 cm.
Larger than Buzzard. Reddish-brown back and long,
forked tail, pale head and long, angled wings with pale
patches on undersides. Effortless soaring flight like
Buzzard's but silhouette is unmistakable with long tail
constantly twisted about as a rudder.
Status
Resident.
Habitat and Range
The Red Kite is confined as a breeding bird to the
hanging oak woods of the steep valleys of central Wales.
There have been recent attempts to increase their range
to parts of England and Scotland.
Nest
High in tree fork, built with sticks, branches, wool and
even rags.
Eggs
Dull white, blotched and streaked with reddish-brown.
Clutch 2-4.
Food
Small mammals and birds, insects and carrion.

Hobby
Falco subbuteo

Hobby

Size and Field Characteristics   30-35 cm.
Size of Kestrel, with shorter tail and longer wings. Flight silhouette can resemble large Swift. Slate-grey upper-parts, head and tail, whitish chin and face with black moustachial stripe. Breast boldly streaked with black and white, reddish undertail, pale grey barred underwing. The male is slightly more colourful than the female.

Status
Summer resident.

Habitat and Range
The open heaths and downs of southern England provide the breeding habitat of the Hobby. In winter, the birds return to Africa.

Nest
Like other falcons does not build a nest, occupies old crow nests usually at a considerable height.

Eggs
Off-white, blotched with reddish-brown. Clutch 2-3.

Food
Capable of taking members of the Swallow family, and young Swifts on the wing. Often seen taking large flying insects such as dragonflies.

Capercaillie
Tetrao urogallus

Capercaillie

Size and Field Characteristics 60-86 cm.
A huge turkey-sized bird. The male is a very large
blackish bird with greenish highlights, white shoulder
patches and red wattles. The tail is fanned during
display when the birds gather at the spring 'leks'. Cocks
utter remarkable 'plip-plopping' call. Females are much
smaller than males but larger than female Black Grouse,
orange-brown in colour, heavily barred in darker shades.
Status
Resident.
Habitat and Range
The old Caledonian Pine Forests and more recent forests
of mature conifers in the north of Scotland.
Nest
A depression scraped among the scant vegetation at the
base of a tree.
Eggs
Creamy, with reddish-brown markings. Clutch 5-8.
Food
Pine shoots, flowers, leaves and berries.

Woodcock
Scolopax rusticola

Woodcock

Size and Field Characteristics   34 cm.
Larger than Lapwing. Distinctive roundish body, upper-
parts patterned with shades of brown, under-parts barred
with cream and brown. Light and dark brown bars
across top of head, short legs and longish bill about one
and a half times length of head. 'Crepuscular', that is,
active during twilight.

Status
Resident and winter visitor.

Habitat and Range
Both broad-leaved woodland and conifer are the haunts
of the Woodcock, where among dead bracken or
brushwood the birds are difficult to locate, being
perfectly camouflaged and reluctant to break cover.
Evening territorial display flight, called 'roding', is good
identification feature. Widespread throughout British
Isles.

Nest
A slight hollow on ground lined with dead leaves,
usually well hidden.

Eggs
Greyish-buff with chestnut and grey markings.
Clutch 4-5.

Food
Earthworms, grubs and insects, probed for in some
damp, soggy area, late evening or early morning.

Red-backed Shrike
Lanius collurio

Red-backed Shrike

Size and Field Characteristics 17 cm.
Smaller than Starling. Perches prominently with upright
stance on bush or telegraph wire, cocking its head as it
searches for prey. Male has reddish-brown back and
wings with darker outer feathers, grey head and rump,
black and white face and tail, pinkish breast and distinct
hooked beak. Female less well marked.

Status
Rare summer resident.

Habitat and Range
Scrubby areas with hawthorn bushes. Almost extinct as
breeding bird in England. Best seen as migrant on east
coast. Winters in Africa.

Nest
A deep cup-shaped structure, well concealed in thorn or
other dense bush. Built with moss, grass, rootlets and
lined with fine fibres.

Eggs
Greyish colour variable from buff to pink, densely
spotted with olive or brown. Clutch 4-6.

Food
Mainly bumble-bees and beetles, small mammals and
birds also taken. The Red-backed Shrike has habit of
storing excess food by impaling victim on thorn in its
'larder', as such places are known.

Great Grey Shrike
Lanius excubitor

Great Grey Shrike

Size and Field Characteristics   24 cm.
Larger than Starling. Perches prominently on top of
bushes or telegraph wires, scanning the ground below
for prey. Grey head, back and rump, black and white
face, wings and long tail, white under-parts, black
hooked beak. Occurs with regularity at favoured
wintering sites.

Status
Winter visitor.

Habitat and Range
Open ground with trees and bushes, scrubby areas and
expanses of ground where conifers have been clear-
felled. Found mainly on the east coast, also regular
inland visitor. Breeds throughout Europe, non-breeder
in British Isles.

Food
Small mammals and birds, large insects. Great Grey
Shrike stores surplus food by impaling prey on hawthorn
spikes; such places are called 'larders'.

Birds of Streams, Ponds, Rivers, Lakes and Lochs

At any point in the British Isles there is always a source of fresh water not too far away. From the highest mountains and hills, where clear running streams provide a habitat for Grey Wagtails and Dippers, to city lakes and ponds where Mallard Duck, Canada Geese and Mute Swans thrive with the aid of a little human support. Between these two extremes, rivers and waterways support many species including the exotic Kingfisher. Highland tarns and lochs are the breeding haunts of Divers and rare Grebes, while other expanses of fresh water throughout the country provide breeding habitat for the more common Grebes, Coots, Moorhens and an assortment of Ducks.

In winter, reservoirs, lakes and lochs provide sanctuary as roosting places for many thousands of wildfowl that arrive in Britain from northern and eastern Europe.

Red-throated Diver
Gavia stellata

Red-throated Diver

Size and Field Characteristics   60 cm.
Similar in size to Mallard. Swims low in water. Bill slightly upturned. The colour of the Red-throated Diver's throat is red only in summer, during which time its head is ashy-grey. In winter the plumage of both sexes is much paler, being grey and white.

Status
Resident

Habitat and Range
In summer, inland freshwater lochs and tarns and esturial coastal waters of north-west Scotland and Ireland. In winter, estuaries and coasts around the British Isles.

Nest
A slight depression among the vegetation near the water's edge, scantily lined with reeds and heather stalks.

Eggs
Elongated. Olive-brown with darker spots and markings. Clutch 2.

Food
Fish, which the Red-throated Diver visits estuaries to catch as breeding tarn is usually too small to provide enough food for young.

Black-throated Diver
Gavia arctica

Black-throated Diver

Size and Field Characteristics   58-73 cm.
Slightly larger than Mallard. In summer the Black-throated Diver has a black throat, ashy-grey head and a black and white chequered appearance on its upper back and wings. In winter it strongly resembles the grey and white winter plumage of the Red-throated Diver, but its bill is straight.

Status
Resident.

Habitat and Range
In summer, freshwater lochs of northern Scotland. In winter, they can be seen further south in coastal waters, mainly in estuaries.

Nest
A slight depression among vegetation near the water's edge, often on a small island, scantily lined with reeds and heather stems.

Eggs
Olive-brown with black spots. Clutch 2.

Food
Almost entirely fish.

Related Species
The Great Northern Diver (*Gavia immer*), at 70-90 cm, most often seen off our north-western coasts, has a dark-green head in summer but in winter plumage it closely resembles our other two Divers.

Great Crested Grebe
Podiceps cristatus

Great Crested Grebe

Size and Field Characteristics   48 cm.
Slightly smaller than Mallard. Sits high in water, dives
frequently. In summer, recognised by its black, spiky
crest and chestnut and black frilly 'tippits'. In winter,
dark grey crown and back, whitish neck and under-parts.
Status
Resident.
Habitat and Range
In summer, reservoirs, lochs, lakes and gravel pits with
suitable vegetated edges. In winter, frequents estuaries.
Widespread throughout the British Isles. Scarce in north
of Scotland, extreme south-east of England and parts of
southern and eastern Ireland.
Nest
Usually a raft-like platform of aquatic vegetation capable
of rising or falling with the water level and anchored by
reed stems.
Eggs
White, soon becoming stained. Clutch 3-6.
Food
Fish, molluscs, crustaceans.
Related Species
The Red-necked Grebe is only a few centimetres smaller,
does not breed in this country. In autumn it can be seen
in summer plumage, black crown, reddish neck, white
chin and cheeks. In winter, its neck and under-parts are
greyish.

Slavonian Grebe
Podiceps auritus

Slavonian Grebe

Size and Field Characteristics 35 cm.
Smaller than Mallard. In summer, striking appearance, chestnut neck and flanks, black head with yellow tufts. In winter, black and white plumage with thin, dark bill.

Status
Resident.

Habitat and Range
In summer, small lochans in north of Scotland where it breeds in small numbers. In winter, sheltered bays and coastal estuaries.

Nest
A platform of floating aquatic vegetation anchored by reed stems or other pond vegetation.

Eggs
White, becoming stained.

Food
Fish, crustaceans.

Related Species
The Black-necked Grebe (*Podiceps nigricollis*), at 32 cm, is another rare bird on some remote Scottish lochans, but in winter, when it is more likely to be seen, its plumage closely resembles that of the Slavonian Grebe but with a darker neck and slightly upturned bill.

Little Grebe
Tachybaptus ruficollis

Little Grebe

Size and Field Characteristics   27 cm.
Smaller than Moorhen. A dumpy little bird with a short
bill. In summer, chestnut cheeks and yellow patch at
base of bill. In winter, grey and black plumage, also
recognised by its small size and shape.
Status
Resident.
Habitat and Range
Freshwater ponds, lakes, lochs, gravel pits and
waterways. Widespread throughout the British Isles
except for the north-west of Scotland.
Nest
A platform of floating aquatic vegetation anchored by a
willow branch or reeds.
Eggs
Creamy-white, soon becoming stained. Clutch 4-6.
Food
Aquatic insects, small crustaceans and fish.

Grey Heron
Ardea cinerea

Grey Heron

Size and Field Characteristics 94 cm.
A large stork-like bird, the Heron has a grey back, a long white neck with black markings and a black wispy crest. It has long legs and a long dagger-like bill. In flight, the head is drawn back and the legs are stretched straight out behind.

Status
Resident.

Habitat and Range
Open meadows with drains and marshy ditches, pond edges and river banks. Widespread throughout the British Isles.

Nest
Usually in tree-top colonies called 'heronries', and occasionally on sea cliffs. A bulky construction of sticks and twigs lined with finer material.

Eggs
Greenish-blue. Clutch 3-5.

Food
Fish, frogs, worms, small mammals and birds.

Bittern
Botaurus stellaris

Bittern

Size and Field Characteristics   70-80 cm.
Smaller than the Grey Heron. The Bittern is a tawny-brown coloured bird, barred and mottled in a darker shade, it has longish legs and a dagger-like bill. Skulks among reeds and often stands with neck, head and beak pointing skywards to avoid detection. The male makes a far-carrying 'booming' sound.

Status
Resident, numbers increased in winter by birds from colder parts of Europe.

Habitat and Range
The reed beds of East Anglia and the R.S.P.B. Reserve at Leighton Moss, Lancashire are the strongholds of the last remaining pairs of Bittern in the British Isles.

Nest
A reedy structure built at ground level among the reeds.

Eggs
Olive-brown. Clutch 4-6.

Food
Mainly fish.

Mute Swan
Cygnus olor

Mute Swan

Size and Field Characteristics 145-160 cm.
Much larger than the Canada Goose, the Mute Swan is
unmistakable with its pure white plumage and its orange
bill which has a black knob at the base. Immature birds
are less attractive in their brownish-grey mottled
plumage.

Status
Resident.

Habitat and Range
Lakes, ponds and slow-moving rivers are the Mute
Swan's domain. Widespread throughout the British Isles
except for mountain ranges and the far north-east of
Scotland.

Nest
A very bulky affair at the water's edge constructed with
sticks, roots, rushes and reeds.

Eggs
Large, greenish-grey. Clutch 6-10.

Food
Water plants, weeds and some amphibia which the Swan
reaches underwater by up-ending.

Whooper Swan
Cygnus cygnus

Whooper Swan

Size and Field Characteristics   145-160 cm.
Similar in size to the Mute Swan. Adults have pure
white plumage and a large pointed yellow patch at the
base of the bill, immature birds closely resemble those of
the Mute Swan. Whoopers tend to hold their necks
straighter than other swans when settled.

Status
Mainly a winter visitor, but a few pairs breed in the far
north of Scotland.

Habitat and Range
Whooper Swans frequent fields by rivers and estuaries,
upland pools and lochs. The south of England and
south Wales are usually shunned by these Icelandic
visitors.

Nest
Like the Mute Swan's, a large construction of sticks,
roots, rushes and reeds.

Eggs
Similar to those of the Mute Swan, large, green grey.
Clutch 6-10.

Food
Water plants and weeds, grain and potatoes.

Bewick's Swan
Cygnus columbianus

Bewick's Swan

Size and Field Characteristics ll5-l25 cm.
The smallest of the three British Swans, the Bewick's adult plumage is recognized by the small rounded yellow patch at the base of the bill, and the slight 'S' shape of its neck when settled on the water.
Status
Winter visitor.
Habitat and Range
Wildfowl reserves, salt marshes, wet meadows and reservoirs throughout England and Solway Firth region, attract this winter visitor from the USSR.
Food
Water plants, grass shoots, grain and potatoes.

Canada Goose
Branta canadensis

Canada Goose

Size and Field Characteristics 95 cm.
The Canada is our largest Goose. It has a black head
and neck with a white throat patch, brown barred back
and pale under-parts. The beak and legs are black.
Status
Resident.
Habitat and Range
Like the Mute Swan and many of our 'wild' Ducks, the
Canada Goose is an opportunist, choosing to take up
residence on ponds and lakes near human habitation.
Widespread throughout most of England, they are much
scarcer in Wales and Scotland.
Nest
On the ground, usually concealed under a willow bush
or other tree or shrub. Built with reeds and grasses and
lined with leaves and down.
Eggs
Creamy-white. Clutch 4-6.
Food
Roots and stems of aquatic plants for which it up-ends;
also grazes.

Observations on Ducks

Generally speaking drakes (males) are more colourful than ducks (females). The ducks are coloured mottled-brown, drab-brown or grey making them more difficult to see as they incubate eggs, either among undergrowth or in holes.

Surface feeders or 'dabbling Ducks', such as Mallard, Teal and Pintail find their food on or near the surface. The tips of their tails are clear of the water when swimming and these ducks, when disturbed, spring clean from the water. Surface feeders also 'up-end' when feeding.

Diving Ducks such as Tufted Duck, Pochard and Goldeneye find their food under the surface and on the lake bottom. Their tails lie on the surface of the water and when disturbed these Ducks patter over the surface before taking-off.

Sea Ducks mostly require a running take-off to get airborne but some, such as the Long-tailed Duck, can spring direct from the surface of the sea.

'Sawbills', namely Goosander, Red-breasted Merganser and Smew, have needle-sharp serrations along the edges of their bills enabling them to catch, hold and devour fish.

In mid-summer, drakes go through an 'eclipse' period, which is most noticeable among the surface feeders, when the drakes lose most of their colour and strongly resemble the plumage of the ducks, retaining only the normal colouring of the wings. At this time the main flight feathers are also moulted, rendering the birds flightless until the feathers re-grow.

The 'speculum' is a bar of bright colour, often with a metallic sheen, along the secondary feathers on the wings of surface feeding Ducks. Some diving Ducks also possess these wing bars, but they are much less prominent in these species.

Wigeon
Anas penelope

Wigeon

Size and Field Characteristics   48 cm.
A surface feeder. Smaller than Mallard. The drake
Wigeon is an attractive little Duck in various shades of
grey, a chestnut head and golden-yellow forehead and
crown. In flight, shows conspicuous white wing patch.
The duck is mottled in shades of brown and grey.
Green speculum. Often seen in large numbers, when
distinctive whistling call can be heard.
Status
Mainly winter visitor, also small resident breeding
population.
Habitat and Range
In winter, birds from Iceland and northern Europe
inhabit salt marshes, pastures and ponds throughout the
British Isles.
Nest
Well concealed among ground vegetation, built with
grasses and down.
Eggs
White. Clutch 6-8.
Food
Grass and aquatic material disturbed from pond bottoms
by up-ending Swans or other Ducks.

Teal
Anas crecca

Teal

Size and Field Characteristics 34-38 cm.
A surface feeder. Much smaller than Mallard, with which
it often associates. The drake is grey with a chestnut
and green head, yellow patch at the base of the tail and
noticeable white stripe on the wing. The duck is a
brown mottled bird with a green speculum. Teal are
very wary little Ducks.
Status
Resident, with numbers greatly increased in winter.
Habitat and Range
Reedy and marshy areas with open patches of shallow
water, and ponds with reed and sedge edges.
Widespread throughout the Briish Isles except for the far
north-west of Scotland.
Nest
Well concealed in heathery tussock or other vegetation,
constructed with grasses, bracken and down.
Eggs
Pale buff. Clutch 8-12.
Food
Water plants and seeds for which it dabbles on the
surface of the water, also insects and worms.

Mallard
Anas platyrhynchos

Mallard

Size and Field Characteristics 65cm.
The most common and widespread of all wild Ducks, it
is instantly recognized. The drake is greyish-brown with
a glossy, dark-green head, white neck ring, purple breast
and white tail. The duck is mottled in shades of brown
and, like the drake, has a violet speculum.
Status
Resident, with numbers greatly increased by northern
and eastern European birds in winter.
Habitat and Range
Mallard are found in practically any watery place
throughout the country, including town and city parks
and ponds.
Nest
Most often concealed among bramble or other dense
undergrowth on the ground, but at times in bowl or
large hole in tree. Built with twigs, grasses, feathers and
lined with down.
Eggs
Pale brownish-white. Clútch 9-14.
Food
Water plants and aquatic creatures in the wild, with
bread scraps and grain readily taken in urban ponds.
The Mallard is a dabbling Duck, or surface feeder, which
up-ends to reach food under the surface.

Gadwall
Anas strepera

Gadwall

Size and Field Characteristics 48-65 cm.
A surface feeder. Smaller than Mallard. The drake
Gadwall is greyish-brown with a black tail and white
speculum which is noticeable in flight. The duck,
although mottled in shades of brown, is readily
recognized by her white speculum.
Status
Resident, with numbers increased in winter by birds
from central Europe.
Habitat and Range
Marshes, lakes and ponds with a good edge of covering
vegetation. Largest numbers found in southern half of
England, mainly around East Anglia, Loch Leven area of
Kinross and parts of southern and eastern Scotland.
Nest
On ground among vegetation near water's edge, built
with sedges, grass and down
Eggs
White. Clutch 8-ll.
Food
Water plants, aquatic insects and seeds for which it
dabbles or up-ends.

Garganey
Anas querquedula

Garganey

Size and Field Characteristics   38-40 cm.
A surface feeder. Smaller than a Mallard. The drake
Garganey has a brown mottled breast and tail end, a
purplish head with broad white eye-stripe, pinkish tinge
to his back, and blue black and white stripes on his
wings, altogether a handsome bird. The duck is mottled
in shades of brown. Garganey, like other surface
feeding Ducks, sit high on the water. Dull-green
speculum.

Status
Summer resident, the only duck in this category in the
British Isles.

Habitat and Range
Shallow flooded areas and water meadows of south-east
England.

Nest
Well concealed in reedy tussock, built with reeds and
lined with down.

Eggs
Pale brownish colour. Clutch 6-8.

Food
Aquatic vegetation and insects for which it dabbles and
up-ends.

Shoveler
Anas clypeata

Shoveler

Size and Field Characteristics 46-50 cm.
A surface feeder. Smaller than a Mallard. The drake
Shoveler has a white body with a broad chestnut band
on the flanks. His back is black with white stripes, and
from his green head protrudes a large paddle-shaped
black bill. The duck is mottled in shades of brown with
similarly shaped bill and green and black speculum.

Status
Resident, with some birds moving south for the winter,
while others from northern Europe take their place.

Habitat and Range
Lakes, lochs and waterways, where it favours the
shallower water. Winters throughout most of England
and the southern half of Scotland, with its breeding
range slightly less widespread.

Nest
A hollow among reeds, often quite open, lined with
grass and down.

Eggs
Buffish. Clutch 8-12.

Food
Tiny molluscs, crustaceans and water plant seeds for
which it sifts the watery mud through its specially
adapted beak.

Pintail
Anas acuta

Pintail

Size and Field Characteristics   54-66 cm, including
approximately 20 cm tail.
About Mallard size. The drake Pintail has a chocolate
coloured head with a white stripe that broadens
downwards to cover his breast. His body is grey, with
black stripes on his wing feathers, his back-end and long
pintail are black. The duck is mottled in shades of
brown. Pintails have noticeably longer necks than all
other surface feeding Ducks. Bronze speculum.
Status
Mainly winter visitor, with a small resident population.
Habitat and Range
Estuaries and coastal mud flats attract thousands of
Pintails from Iceland and northern Europe in winter. A
few pairs breed in East Anglia.
Nest
Usually situated in grassy or heather tussock, built with
the same material and lined with down.
Eggs
Yellowish-cream. Clutch 6-l0.
Food
Because of the Pintail's longer neck it can reach water
plants and snails at a greater depth than other surface
feeding Duck, while up-ending.

Pochard
Aythya ferina

Pochard

Size and Field Characteristics 42-48 cm.
A diving Duck. Smaller than Mallard. The drake
Pochard, with his chestnut-coloured head, black breast
and tail-end, and greyish body, is easily recognized. The
duck is coloured greyish-brown.
Status
Mainly winter visitor, with a small number of resident
breeding pairs.
Habitat and Range
In winter, when numbers from Central Europe arrive,
they favour lakes, reservoirs, lochs and ponds. In
summer, expanses of fresh water with a good reed fringe
are selected. Breeding pairs found mainly in south-east
England.
Nest
Usually concealed among vegetation near water. Built
with grasses and lined with down.
Eggs
Greenish-grey. Clutch 6-12.
Food
Dives for waterplant seeds, insect larvae and shellfish.

Tufted Duck
Aythya fuligula

Tufted Duck

Size and Field Characteristics   40-46 cm.
Smaller than Mallard. A diving Duck. The drake Tufted
Duck is black with white flanks and belly, and a
drooping crest. The duck is brown with paler flanks.
Both birds have a white wing bar, noticeable in flight.
Status
Resident, numbers increased in winter by birds from
Iceland and northern Europe.
Habitat and Range
Lochs, lakes and reservoirs, gravel pits, rivers and urban
ponds. Widespread except for parts of the north-west of
Scotland.
Nest
Well concealed among vegetation by the water's edge,
built with grasses and down.
Eggs
Greenish-grey. Clutch 7-12.
Food
Molluscs, crustaceans and small fish, which are procured
during dives lasting about twenty seconds.

Mandarin
Aix galericulata

Mandarin

Size and Field Characteristics 42-48 cm.
The drake Mandarin is a multi-coloured Duck with a dark, glossy-green head crown, breast, back and tail end. He has a broad white eye-stripe, pale orange flanks and bright orange 'side whiskers' and 'sail' feathers. The duck has a grey head with white eye ring and stripe, a brown back and distinct brown and white marbling on her breast and flank.

Status
Resident.

Habitat and Range
Lakes and lochs with woodland edge. Mostly seen in wildfowl collections, with breeding population of south-east England and central Scotland descended from escapees.

Nest
Hole in tree. No material added except Duck down.

Eggs
Buffish-white. Clutch 8-12.

Food
Water plants and seeds, molluscs.

Related Species
The Ruddy Duck (*Oxyura jamaicensis*), at 38 cm, is another Duck established in the wild from collections. The drake has a chestnut body, dark-green head and tail, and conspicuous white face patch and back end. The duck's plumage is shades of brown with a dark brown cap.

Red-crested Pochard
Netta rufina

Red-crested Pochard

Size and Field Characteristics   53-56 cm.
Smaller than Mallard. The drake Red-crested Pochard
has an orangey-red head, black breast, under-parts and
tail, pinkish-fawn back and white flanks. The duck is
pale brown with white cheeks and throat. Both sexes
have prominent white wing-bars.
Status
Resident and winter visitor.
Habitat and Range
Mostly seen in wildfowl collections. Escapees and their
descendants can be found breeding in the southern half
of England. Winter visitors in small numbers from,
USSR.
Nest
Well concealed among ground vegetation, usually on an
island, built with twigs and reeds, lined with down.
Eggs
Brownish-olive. Clutch 6-l0.
Food
Red-crested Pochard both dabble on the surface and
dive under it for food. Mainly water plants and seeds.
Related Species
The Ferruginous Duck (*Aythya nyroca*), at 40 cm, is
smaller than a Mallard. The drake has a deep-chestnut
head, breast and flanks. The duck is chocolate-brown.
Both have dark-brown backs and a white patch at the
base of the tail. Most birds seen in the wild are
escapees, but a few are truly winter visitors.

Goldeneye
Bucephala clangula

Goldeneye

Size and Field Characteristics 42-48 cm.
Smaller than Mallard. The drake Goldeneye is black and white, with characteristic glossy dark-green 'buffel' head in which are set the golden-coloured eyes that give the bird its name. It also has white patches at the base of the bill. The duck has a chocolate-brown head with the rest of her plumage grey and white.

Status
Mainly winter visitor, also regular breeder.

Habitat and Range
In winter, thousands of Goldeneye from USSR and Scandinavia inhabit inland lochs and reservoirs and other expanses of water throughout Britain. They can also be seen in coastal waters. In central Scotland breeding birds show a preference for tree-lined lochs.

Nest
Usually a tree hole, but readily accept nest-boxes. Material: feathers and down.

Eggs
Bluish-green. Clutch 7-12.

Food
Crustaceans, molluscs and aquatic insects, which the birds dive to a fair depth then overturn stones to procure.

Smew
Mergus albellus

Smew

Size and Field Characteristics 38-44 cm.
Much smaller than Mallard. The drake Smew is a little
white Duck with greyish wingtips, rump and tail. He
has a black eyepatch, black streaks down his back and
other black lines. The duck is grey with reddish-brown
head, white cheeks and throat. Both sexes display black
and white wing pattern in flight.

Status
Winter visitor.

Habitat and Range
Freshwater lochs, lakes, reservoirs and gravel pits. The
Smew, a migrant from USSR, is absent throughout most
of the British Isles, the largest concentration of l00-200
birds frequenting the south-east of England.

Food
Smew are 'sawbills', Ducks that have serrated edges to
their bills, which enable them to catch and hold their
fishy diet, which is brought to the surface to be
devoured.

Red-breasted Merganser
Mergus serrator

Red-breasted Merganser

Size and Field Characteristics 52-58 cm.
Slightly smaller than Mallard. The drake Red-breasted Merganser has a dark green head with a wispy double crest, a mottled chestnut breast, white collar and black, white and grey body. The duck is greyish with brownish head and crest. Mergansers swim low in the water.

Status
Resident, numbers increased in winter.

Habitat and Range
Lochs, rivers and coastal waters of Scotland, Ireland and down the west coast to north Wales. In winter, also southern and eastern coastal waters.

Nest
Usually under overhang in bank, or well concealed among undergrowth, grass and down lined.

Eggs
Greenish-buff. Clutch 6-l0.

Food
Red-breasted Mergansers are 'sawbills', having long thin bills with serrated edges with which they procure and hold their fish prey. Occasionally fish in packs.

Goosander
Mergus merganser

Goosander

Size and Field Characteristics   58-65 cm.
Size of Mallard. The largest of the three British
'sawbills'. The drake Goosander has a glossy dark green
head, black back, grey tail and salmon-pink breast and
under-parts. The duck is grey with a shaggy brown
head. Goosanders swim low in the water.
Status
Resident.
Habitat and Range
Practically the whole of Scotland, the north of England
and central Wales are the breeding haunts of the
Goosander, where it can be found on freshwater lochs,
reservoirs and rivers. In winter, also coastal in some
sheltered estuaries.
Nest
Usually hole in tree, with no material added apart from
duck down.
Eggs
Creamy-white. Clutch 6-12.
Food
The longish bill of the Goosander, with serrated edges,
is ideal for catching and holding fish, the diet of these
underwater anglers.

Osprey
Pandion haliaetus

Osprey

Size and Field Characteristics 56-60 cm.
Slightly larger than Buzzard. Dark brown on upper-parts
with a broad band of dark brown along side of white
face, slight crest, white under-parts with dark brown
wing patches and tips. Soars on noticeably longer wings
than those of Buzzard.

Status
Summer resident.

Habitat and Range
Scottish lochs and estuaries, gradually spreading further
south in its breeding range. In England, seen as migrant
in spring and autumn, moving to and from wintering
grounds in Africa.

Nest
Usually situated atop pine tree, at times conspicuous but
normally well concealed in canopy, bulky, built with
sticks, branches, bracken and grasses. Some nests used
year after year.

Eggs
Creamy, blotched with reddish-brown. Clutch 2-4.

Food
Ospreys plunge feet-first into the water to grasp their
fish prey. Specially adapted talons ensure that few
escape.

Water Rail
Rallus aquaticus

Water Rail

Size and Field Characteristics   24-28 cm.
Smaller than Moorhen. From head to back-end cone-
shaped, ideal for poking its way through dense
vegetation. Upper-parts brown with black streaks, face,
breast and under-parts bluish-grey, black and white
barring on flanks, longish down-curved red bill.
Status
Resident.
Habitat and Range
Dense reed beds, overgrown ditches and marshes are
the haunts of the Water Rail, where it is more often
heard than seen, due to elusive nature. Widespread
throughout most of England, the south of Wales and the
southern half of Scotland where the habitat is suitable.
Nest
Platform of reeds lined with dead leaves, concealed in
clump of reeds.
Eggs
Light buff, lightly spotted with dark-brown. Clutch 7-ll.
Food
Mainly freshwater animal life. Grain and even offal in
winter.
Related Species
The Spotted Crake (*Porzana porzana*), at 23 cm, closely
resembling the Water Rail in colouring and found in
similar habitat, is slightly smaller with noticeably shorter
bill. A scarce summer resident and autumn migrant.

Moorhen
Gallinula chloropus

Moorhen

Size and Field Characteristics 32-24 cm.
Much smaller than Mallard. Appears black and white at
a distance, at close range bluish tinge to head, neck and
under-parts, brownish back with white line along flanks
and white sides to tail. Red frontal shield and beak with
yellow tip. Sexes similar.
Status
Resident.
Habitat and Range
Ponds, lochs, gravel pits, ditches and other expanses of
freshwater with reedy fringe. Widespread throughout
the British Isles except for north-west of Scotland.
Nest
Platform of reeds and sedges among reeds, or built on
some submerged object, at times quite obvious.
Eggs
Buffish, blotched and spotted with brown. Clutch 5-12.
Food
Water plants, weeds and insects.

Coot
Fulica atra

Coot

Size and Field Characteristics   36-38 cm.
Larger than Moorhen. A black-plumaged water bird with
conspicuous white frontal shield at base of bill.
Extremely quarrelsome in breeding season. Gregarious
in winter, large numbers congregating on larger lakes
when smaller ones freeze over.
Status
Resident.
Habitat and Range
Reservoirs, lakes, ponds, gravel pits with reed or sedge
fringe. Widespread throughout the British Isles except
for north-west Scotland.
Nest
A bulky construction of sedges, reeds and other
vegetation, usually in reed bed.
Eggs
Stone-coloured with blackish spots. Clutch 4-10.
Food
Mainly aquatic vegetation and insects.

Oystercatcher
Haematopus ostralegus

Oystercatcher

Size and Field Characteristics 40-44 cm.
Larger than Lapwing. Black upper-parts and breast,
white under-parts and wing bar. Pinkish legs, orange
bill slightly longer than length of head.
Status
Resident, winters in estuaries in large numbers.
Habitat and Range
In summer, coastal and inland river gravel beds and
arable fields. Widespread throughout the whole of
Scotland. Absent from most of inland south-west
England and Wales. In winter, many thousands arrive
from northern countries to join local birds, when they
frequent the entire British coastline.
Nest
A slight depression on gravel or soil.
Eggs
Buffish marked with black spots. Clutch 3-4.
Food
On estuaries mainly molluscs. Inland, worms and
caterpillars.

Ringed Plover
Charadrius biaticula

Ringed Plover

Size and Field Characteristics   20 cm.
Much smaller than Lapwing. Black, white and brown
head, pale brown above, white collar and under-parts,
black breast band, white wing bar, short legs, yellow
and black bill shorter than length of head.
Status
Resident.
Habitat and Range
In summer, shingly coasts and inland river courses are
breeding haunts. In winter, coasts and estuaries.
Migrating birds pass through British Isles from wintering
grounds in Africa.
Nest
Shallow depression among small pebbles, or scrape in
bare soil.
Eggs
Buff, with brownish black spots. Clutch 3-4.
Food
Small molluscs and crustaceans, worms and insects.
Related Species
The Little Ringed Plover (*Charadrius dubius*), at l5 cm,
is daintier than Ringed Plover. Similar colours but has
white line across head, distinct yellow eye-rings and
shows no white wing bar in flight. Summer resident to
many parts of England, where it breeds on extensive
gravel scrapes.

Common Sandpiper
Actitis hypoleucos

Common Sandpiper

Size and Field Characteristics   20 cm.
Larger than Ringed Plover. Brown upper-parts, white belly
and undertail. Brownish streaked breast, shows faint
white wing bar in flight, greenish legs, and short straight
beak about length of head. Bobs tail walking.

Status
Mainly summer resident.

Habitat and Range
Hill streams, river courses, loch and reservoir edges are
the haunts of the Common Sandpiper in Scotland, Wales
and north of England. On migration to and from African
wintering grounds, can be seen throughout British Isles.
Odd birds winter in extreme south-west of country.

Nest
A well-concealed, neat cup of fine grasses, on the ground
under a broad-leaved plant or in a grassy bank.

Eggs
Buffish, with dark brown spots. Clutch 4.

Food
Small invertebrates and vegetable matter.

Related Species
The Wood Sandpiper (*Tringa glareola*) is darker on
upper-parts and has longer legs. Mainly a bird of
passage, favouring the east coast, a few pairs breed in
north of Scotland. The Green Sandpiper (*Tringa
ochropus*), darker on upper-parts than both Common and
Wood, has white rump in flight, and is seen mainly as an
autumn migrant.

Kingfisher
Alcedo attbis

Kingfisher

Size and Field Characteristics   17 cm, including 4 cm
bill. Smaller than a Starling. Colourful and shy.
Greenish-blue head and wings spotted with bright blue,
bright blue back and tail, chestnut-orange under-parts,
white patch on throat and sides of neck. Short red legs,
long dagger-like bill the length of head. Flight is fast
and low over water, veers widely or rises to treetop level
when encountering an intruder.

Status
Resident.

Habitat and Range
Clear running streams, rivers and lakes are the breeding
haunts of the Kingfisher. In winter, they may move
downstream as far as coastal estuaries. Widespread
throughout England and Wales and as far north as the
central belt of Scotland.

Nest
Small chamber at the end of a tunnel about one metre in
length, which is fashioned by the Kingfisher burrowing
into sandy bank above water.

Eggs
White. Clutch 5-8.

Food
Sticklebacks, bullheads, minnows and other small fish
are sought by the Kingfisher, pounced on from an
overhanging branch or other perch, and occasionally
from a hovering position.

Sand Martin
Riparia riparia

Sand Martin

Size and Field Characteristics   12 cm.
Smaller than Swallow. Brown upper-parts and breast
band, rest of under-parts white, pointed wings, forked
tail, has a more erratic flight than Swallow or House
Martin.
Status
Summer resident, one of the first to arrive.
Habitat and Range
May be seen flying above rivers, ponds and large
expanses of water throughout most of the British Isles.
In autumn, Sand Martins gather on telegraph wires and
roost collectively in reed beds prior to leaving for south
African wintering grounds.
Nest
In colonies. Most often a burrow in a sandy bank of
river or stream, or face of sand quarry, which the birds
excavate for up to two metres before lining small
chamber with bits of straw and feathers. Occasionally
nests in pipes.
Eggs
White. Clutch 4-6.
Food
Flying insects, caught by Sand Martin skimming low over
water or at higher levels.

Pied Wagtail
Motacilla alba

Pied Wagtail

Size and Field Characteristics 18 cm, including long tail.
A dainty, slim little bird with a long tail which is constantly wagged. Male has distinct black and white plumage, mainly black upper-parts and white under-parts. Female is greyer on back. Roosts communally in winter in reed beds or on buildings.

Status
Resident.

Habitat and Range
Farmland, parkland, open country, usually but not always near water. Widespread throughout British Isles.

Nest
Built with twigs, moss and grass, lined with hair and feathers. Located in hole in wall, crevice, pipe or outbuilding.

Eggs
White flecked with grey. Clutch 4-6.

Food
Seeds, and insects, which are caught by Wagtail chasing erratically over short grass or stones.

Related Species
The European or White Wagtail, paler than female Pied, appears in Britain as passage migrant in spring and autumn.

Yellow Wagtail
Motacilla flava

Yellow Wagtail

Size and Field Characteristics   16.5 cm.
Smaller than Pied or Grey Wagtail. Male has greenish-yellow upper-parts, dark grey wings with double, white wingbars, bright yellow face and under-parts. Female slightly duller.

Status
Summer resident.

Habitat and Range
Wet meadows and lowland pasture beside water, throughout most of England but only a foothold in Wales and Scotland.

Nest
Concealed on ground in grassy tussock, built with bents, grasses and hair.

Eggs
Greyish-white, faintly spotted with brown. Clutch 5-6.

Food
Mainly insects, many taken from ground when disturbed by moving cattle.

Grey Wagtail
Motacilla cinerea

Grey Wagtail

Size and Field Characteristics   l8 cm.
Size of Pied Wagtail. Long tail which is constantly
wagged, often mistaken for Yellow Wagtail. Male has
bluish-grey head and mantle, blackish wings and tail,
bright yellow under-parts with distinct black bib.
Female lacks black bib, having whitish throat.

Status
Resident.

Habitat and Range
Hill burns, streams and clear-running rivers are the
haunts of the Grey Wagtail. Moving to lower reaches in
winter. Found throughout the British Isles, apart from
parts of eastern England.

Nest
Concealed in hollow under overhang in bank of stream,
occasionally built away from water. Built with moss,
leaves, roots and fibres.

Eggs
Buffish, speckled with greyish brown. Clutch 4-6.

Food
Almost entirely insects, picked from among the gravel at
waterside, and from the air above the water, in Hawk-
like fashion.

Dipper
Cinclus cinclus

Dipper

Size and Field Characteristics   18 cm.
Smaller than Starling. A dumpy little bird that stands on
a stone mid-stream, bobbing and dipping, hence its
name. Upper-parts and undertail brownish-black,
chestnut band separates white throat from dark
undertail, powerful black legs and feet.

Status
Resident.

Habitat and Range
Fast-flowing hill burns and rivers throughout Scotland
and Wales, the north and south-west corner of England.
In severe cold weather may move downstream,
occasionally as far as estuaries.

Nest
A domed structure built with moss and grass and lined
with dead leaves, concealed among roots of overhanging
bank, rocky ledge, at times behind waterfall or under
bridge.

Eggs
White. Clutch 3-6.

Food
Aquatic crustaceans, insects and small fish, which the
Dipper catches as it walks and swims under the surface
of the water.

Reed Warbler
Acrocephalus scirpaceus

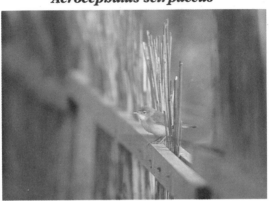

Reed Warbler

Size and Field Characteristics 12.5 cm.
Smaller than Chaffinch. Plain brown upper-parts with paler under-parts. Often nests in loose colonies.

Status
Summer resident.

Habitat and Range
Dense reed beds of southern England and Wales. Winters in Africa.

Nest
A deep cup-shaped structure, woven with grasses around reed stems protruding from water.

Eggs
Pale green speckled with grey. Clutch 3-4.

Food
Insects.

Related Species
The Marsh Warbler (*Acrocephalus palustris*) is of similar size and plumage to Reed Warbler. A rare summer resident, nests in dense vegetation near water, distinguished from Reed Warbler by its song, which is prone to mimicry. Cetti's Warbler (*Cettia cetti*) is another plain-plumaged Warbler, chestnut-brown upper-parts with paler under-parts. A more robustly built Warbler, Cetti's Warbler is a resident species in south-eastern England, where it finds the dense, scrubby vegetation by the waterside to its liking. Being insectivorous, Cetti's Warbler is vulnerable during severe winters.

Sedge Warbler
Acrocephalus schoenobaenus

Sedge Warbler

Size and Field Characteristics 13 cm.
Smaller than Chaffinch. Male has back streaked in
shades of brown, white eye-stripe and orange rump and
pale under-parts. Female is more uniform in colour.
When in territory, often climbs to top of reed stem or
perches prominently on willow bush to observe
intruders.
Status
Summer resident.
Habitat and Range
Damp areas with reed beds, willow-edged rivers,
patches of rosebay willow-herb, or other dense
vegetation near water. Widespread throughout British
Isles except for north-west Scotland. Winters in Africa.
Nest
Built among dense stalks about half a metre from
ground, made with reeds and grasses.
Eggs
Light stone colour, speckled greyish-brown. Clutch 5-6.
Food
Inscts and their larvae.
Related Species
The Grasshopper Warbler (*Locustella naevia*), similar in
size, also has brown streaked plumage, the most difficult
of all Warblers to observe because of skulking habits.
Characteristic 'reeling' song is unmistakable, and best
identification feature.

Bearded Tit
Panurus biarmicus

Bearded Tit

Size and Field Characteristics   16.5 cm.
Longer than Chaffinch. Old name of 'Bearded Reedling'
is more apt as the Bearded Tit is not related to the Tit
family. Back and long tail orange-brown, distinct black,
white and chestnut wings. Male has bluish-grey head
and black 'moustache', female's head is brown.
Status
Resident.
Habitat and Range
Reedbeds of East Anglia and south-east England. Slight
westerly movement in winter.
Nest
A cup-shaped structure built with reeds and grasses,
situated low among dense reeds.
Eggs
White with tiny streaks of purplish-brown. Clutch 5-7.
Food
Mainly insects in summer, in winter, small water snails
and reed seeds. Bearded Tits are vulnerable to severely
cold winters.

Birds of the Sea, Shore, Cliffs and Islands

The waters around the coast of the British Isles support vast numbers of sea birds, huge colonies of Gannets, Guillemots, Puffins, Kittiwakes and Terns and, to a lesser degree, Cormorants, Shag and Sea Duck. Between them they raise millions of young annually on an abundance of assorted sea fish.

Many cliff-nesting sea birds spend the winter months on the open sea, and at this time huge 'rafts' of Sea Duck may be seen, bobbing about on the surface between exploratory dives in pursuit of their maritime diet.

One of the most spectacular sights in the bird world is portrayed by feeding Gannets, thousands gather in the air above a shoal of fish, dive from varying heights, forming an arrowlike shape with their wings a split-second before plunging under the surface.

Manx Shearwater
Puffinus puffinus

Manx Shearwater

Size and Field Characteristics   30-38 cm.
Much smaller than Herring Gull. Black back, wings and
tail. White under-parts. It has a stiff-winged flight
interspersed with glides as it skims low over the waves.
Status
Resident, winters at sea.
Habitat and Range
Feeds on the open sea. Breeds on islands mainly on the
west coast, leaving and returning to the colony during
darkness.
Nest
A burrow in earth.
Eggs
White. Clutch l.
Food
Fish.
Related Species
The Sooty Shearwater (*Puffinus griseus*), at 40-50 cm,
has dark under-parts and is slightly larger than the Manx
Shearwater, and, though they can be seen around British
shores during the summer months, they do not breed in
the British Isles.

Storm Petrel
Hydrobates pelagicus

Storm Petrel

Size and Field Characteristics 16 cm.
Similar in size to Chaffinch. A small black bird with
white rump and square tail. Appears to walk on water,
fluttering its wings as it picks tiny morsels from the
surface of the water. Follows in the wake of ships.
Status
Resident and oceanic.
Habitat and Range
Feeds at sea, breeds in large colonies on remote islands
off northern and western shores of Scotland and Ireland.
Nest
A burrow in the ground, holes in walls or among
boulders.
Eggs
White. Clutch l
Food
Small fish, plankton.
Related Species
The Leach's Petrel (*Oceanodroma leucorrhoa*), at 20 cm,
is slightly larger than the Storm Petrel, with a less
conspicuous white rump and distinct forked tail. Breeds
on the remotest islands of the Outer Hebrides, and feeds
on plankton and small fish. Unlike the Storm Petrel it is
more solitary, avoiding passing ships.

Fulmar
Fulmarus glacialis

Fulmar

Size and Field Characteristics 47 cm.
Smaller than Herring Gull. White head and under-parts,
grey wings and back. Peculiar tubed bill. Recognised in
the air by its stiff-winged, gliding flight.
Status
Resident and oceanic.
Habitat and Range
In summer, sea cliffs around most of the British Isles. In
winter, Fulmars are oceanic, spending their time on the
open sea.
Nest
A bare, rocky ledge or depression on a steep grassy
slope.
Eggs
White. Clutch l.
Food
Fish and fish offal.

Gannet
Sula bassana

Gannet

Size and Field Characteristics 95 cm.
Larger than Herring Gull. The Gannet has long pointed white wings with black tips, spanning almost two metres, a pointed tail and dagger-like bill. Juveniles are greyish-brown on leaving the nest, gradually attaining adult plumage over a period of four years.

Status
Resident and oceanic in winter.

Habitat and Range
Sea cliffs on remote islands, mainly off the Scottish coasts, where colonies include St Kilda, whose numbers total over 58,000 pairs, making it the largest gannetry in the world.

Nest
A bulky affair built with seaweed and grasses.

Eggs
White becoming stained. Clutch l, ocasionally 2.

Food
Fish, for which it dives into the sea in a spectacular fashion.

Cormorant
Phalacrocorax carbo

Cormorant

Size and Field Characteristics   80-100 cm.
Much larger than Herring Gull, the Cormorant is a
blackish-coloured bird with a long neck, white throat
patch and heavy bill. Often seen standing upright on a
post or rock 'spreadeagle' fashion. In summer, both
sexes have shaggy crests and white patches on their
thighs which are absent in winter.
Status
Resident.
Habitat and Range
A bird of the coasts and estuaries around the British
Isles, but scarce on some eastern stretches, also
frequents some inland waters.
Nest
A bulky construction of twigs and seaweed lined with
finer material. Built on rocks on the coast or in trees on
islands on inland lochs.
Eggs
Pale blue, soon becoming covered with a layer of white
chalk. Clutch 3-4.
Food
Fish, mainly from the seabed.

Shag
Phalacrocorax aristotelis

Shag

Size and Field Characteristics 75 cm.
Sometimes called the Green Cormorant the Shag is smaller than the Cormorant and greener in appearance with a thinner neck and finer bill. Both sexes have a shaggy crest during the breeding season, which is absent at other times of the year.

Status
Resident.

Habitat and Range
Rocky coasts and islands around the British Isles except for the south-east corner. Unlike the Cormorant the Shag is seldom seen inland.

Nest
Usually built on a rocky ledge or outcrop, it is a bulky affair made with sticks, seaweed and other vegetation.

Eggs
Pale blue, soon becoming covered with a layer of white chalk. Clutch 3-4.

Food
Does not compete with Cormorant as it fishes in mid-water for 'round' fish, and sandeels.

Brent Goose
Branta bernicla

Brent Goose

Size and Field Characteristics   55-60 cm.
Much smaller than Canada Goose. A very dark-coloured
little Goose similar in length to a Mallard but of heavier
build, it has a black head, neck and chest, black beak
and legs. There are two distinct races, a dark-bellied
race and a pale-bellied race.
Status
Winter visitor.
Habitat and Range
Mud flats of coasts and estuaries. The dark-bellied race
from the USSR winter in the south, the pale-bellied from
Spitzbergen winter on the Northumberland coast, other
pale-bellied birds from Greenland winter in Ireland.
Food
The main food source of the Brent Goose is eel-grass,
the availability of which greatly affects their numbers.

Shelduck
Tadorna tadorna

Shelduck

Size and Field Characteristics 68 cm.
Larger than Mallard. A large white duck with a dark green head, neck and wing patches, it has a chestnut breast-band, red bill and pink legs. The drake has a red knob at the base of the bill.
Status
Resident.
Habitat and Range
Sandy and muddy shores all round the British coast, also lochs, reservoirs and other expanses of water.
Nest
Mostly in rabbit hole, or burrow, in sand dunes, also tree holes and other sites inland. Constructed with grasses and down.
Eggs
Creamy-white. Clutch 8-14.
Food
Molluscs, marine crustaceans and insects.

Scaup
Aythya marila

Scaup

Size and Field Characteristics   42-47 cm.
Smaller than Mallard. A diving Duck, the drake Scaup
has a dark green, almost black, head, breast and tail,
grey back and white flanks. The duck is brownish on
the head and breast with a white patch at the base of the
bill.
Status
Winter visitor.
Habitat and Range
Scaup are Sea Ducks from Iceland and northern Europe
that winter around the shores of the British Isles,
favouring some of the major estuaries.
Food
Waste grain from breweries around the Firth of Forth
attracted many thousands of Scaup in days gone by,
nowadays this food source has ceased to exist so birds
in much smaller numbers rely mainly on molluscs to
sustain them.

Eider
Somateria mollissima

Eider

Size and Field Characteristics 60'cm.
Size of Mallard. The drake Eider has a pure white
mantle and white breast tinged with pink. His crown,
flanks, tail and under-parts are black, the sides of his
head and nape have greenish patches. The wedge-
shaped bill is also a greenish colour. The duck is
dressed in a pattern of buff, brown and black bars and
markings.

Status
Resident.

Habitat and Range
Eiders, being Sea Ducks, spend most of their time on the
open sea, but come ashore to rest on rocky islets or
ledges at the base of cliffs. Breeds around rocky shores
and islands of the north-east coast of the British Isles, it
may be seen further south in winter.

Nest
Usually a grassy tussock or cleft in the rocks, the eggs
are bedded in down which the duck plucks from her
own breast (eiderdown).

Eggs
Creamy coloured. Clutch 4-6.

Food
Mussels and crustaceans, which they can dive to a depth
of about six metres to procure.

Long-tailed Duck
Clangula byemalis

Long-tailed Duck

Size and Field Characteristics   40-46 cm.
Smaller than Mallard, but tail can add l0 cm. Drake has
pied appearance, showing more white on head, neck
and back than duck, both birds have distinctive long
tails. Unlike other diving Ducks does not patter over the
surface of the water on take-off, but springs clean from
the water in similar fashion to surface feeders.
Status
Winter visitor.
Habitat and Range
A northern breeding species, the Long-tailed Duck
mainly visits the inshore waters of the north-east coast of
the British Isles. The Moray Firth area holds thousands
of these spectacular Sea Ducks throughout the winter
months.
Food
Shellfish are the main food items of the Long-tailed
Duck, which it dives under the surface to a depth of up
to 20 metres to procure from the sea bed.

Common Scoter
Melanitta nigra

Common Scoter

Size and Field Characteristics 50 cm.
Smaller than Mallard. The drake Common Scoter is the only Duck whose plumage is entirely black. The duck's plumage is dark brown with paler cheeks.

Status
Mainly winter visitor, with small breeding population.

Habitat and Range
Scoters are Ducks of the open sea, that winter in British waters mainly as visitors from northern Europe and Iceland. Also seen in smaller numbers inland on lochs and reservoirs, especially after storms. Small numbers breed in the extreme north-east of Scotland.

Nest
Well-concealed among vegetation near water's edge, built with grasses and down.

Eggs
Pale-brown. Clutch 6-8.

Food
Molluscs, for which it dives to the seabed.

Related Species
The Velvet Scoter (*Melanitta fusca*) is slightly larger than the Common Scoter, in whose company it can be seen, when the white wing-patches of the Velvet Scoter can be observed, otherwise their plumage is similar. Velvet Scoters do not breed in the British Isles but are regular winter visitors from northern Europe.

Knot
Calidris canutus

Knot

Size and Field Characteristics   24 cm.
Larger than Ringed Plover. A robust little wader.
Greyish upper-parts, white under-parts flecked with
grey, short black legs, and black bill similar in length to
length of head, this is winter plumage of Knot. Usually
seen in large numbers, a huge pack in winter sunlight
twist and turn with great speed, appearing black one
moment then white the next.

Status
Winter visitor and passage migrant.

Habitat and Range
Hundreds of thousands of Knot from the Canadian North
and Greenland winter on British estuaries and stretches
of rocky coastline.

Food
Small crustaceans, molluscs and marine insects.

Related Species
The Sanderling (*Calidris alba*) is slightly larger than
Ringed Plover. Grey upper-parts, white under-parts,
black legs and short black bill describe the Sanderling as
it appears on British coasts throughout the winter. An
extremely active little wader while feeding, chasing
receding waves to pick up tiny shrimps deposited on
sand.

Dunlin
Calidris alpina

Dunlin

Size and Field Characteristics 18 cm.
Smaller than Ringed Plover. In summer, orange-brown
and black mottled upper-parts, grey and brown streaked
breast, black belly and whitish under tail, bill slightly
longer than length of head and slightly down-curved. In
winter, grey-brown upper-parts, whitish underneath with
greyish breast. A short-legged dumpy little wader.
Status
Resident, but mainly winter visitor and passage migrant.
Habitat and Range
High moors with lochs and tarns, and other expanses of
water, are the breeding haunts of Dunlin in the British
Isles. British breeders move south for winter as many
thousands arrive from USSR and Scandinavia to winter
on British estuaries.
Nest
Scrape on ground among low vegetation.
Eggs
Buffish, variably spotted with shades of brown. Clutch
4.
Food
Mainly insects in breeding territory, tiny molluscs and
crustaceans on shore.

Little Stint
Calidris minuta

Little Stint

Size and Field Characteristics 13 cm.
Smaller than Ringed Plover. Smallest British wader.
Chequered chestnut, buff and dark brown upper-parts,
buffish breast and white under-parts, short black legs
and short straight bill shorter than length of head. A tiny
Wader which can be quite tame.
Status
Passage migrant.
Habitat and Range
Muddy coastal estuaries, sewage farms, inland areas of
shallow muddy water. Mainly a visitor to the east coast
in autumn on passage from northern Europe to Africa,
also found inland, mainly southern half of England, on
occasion further north.
Food
Small aquatic invertebrates, picked from the surface of
the mud with rapid head movement.

Turnstone
Arenaria interpres

Turnstone

Size and Field Characteristics   23 cm.
Larger than Ringed Plover. In summer, back is patterned
with black and chestnut, head black and white, white
under-parts. In winter, back and head blackish. Short
orange legs, short stout black bill less than length of
head. From a distance Turnstone looks like a small
Oystercatcher.
Status
Winter visitor and passage migrant.
Habitat and Range
A bird of the shoreline around the coast of the British
Isles. Winter visitors from northern Canada and
Greenland, Scandinavian birds pass along British coasts,
en route to and from African wintering grounds, in
spring and autumn.
Food
Turnstones turn over pebbles and drifts of seaweed in
their search for marine invertebrates, thus finding a food
source missed by other waders.

Purple Sandpiper
Calidris maritima

Purple Sandpiper

Size and Field Characteristics   21 cm.
Larger than Ringed Plover. A dumpy and unusually
tame little wader. Dark greyish-brown upper-parts, dark
grey breast and paler under-parts. Short yellow legs, the
bill is slightly downcurved, yellowish at the base and
about the same length as head. Difficult to spot on
seaweed-covered rocky ledges.

Status
Winter visitor and passage migrant.

Habitat and Range
Rocky coasts of the Orkneys and Shetlands, mainland
Scotland and north-east England, support Purple
Sandpipers from Scandinavia and Greenland.

Nest
Small marine invertebrates.

Related Species
The Curlew Sandpiper (*Calidris ferruginea*) is larger
than Ringed Plover. A greyish-brown-backed little
wader with chestnut tinged under-parts. Slightly
downcurved bill gives it appearance of Dunlin but
Curlew Sandpiper's longer legs avoid confusion.
Passage migrant seen mainly on eastern shores, where it
wades up to its belly while probing for small marine
worms and other invertebrates.

Black-tailed Godwit
Limosa limosa

Black-tailed Godwit

Size and Field Characteristics   40 cm.
Larger than Lapwing. In summer, head, mantle and breast are reddish-brown, wings greyish-brown, belly white. Long legs which project beyond tail in flight, long straight bill fully twice the length of head. In winter, head, breast and upper-parts are grey.

Status
Mainly winter visitor with small breeding population.

Habitat and Range
Icelandic birds winter on British estuaries. The small breeding population of East Anglia winter in Africa.

Nest
A scantily-lined hollow in grass.

Eggs
Olive blotched with brown. Clutch 3-5.

Food
Worms, grubs and other invertebrates.

Related Species
The Bar-tailed Godwit (*Limosa lapponica*) is slightly smaller than Black-tailed Godwit. During spring migration, when birds are seen on south-east coast en-route from Africa to high Arctic breeding grounds, plumage is deep-red. Bar-tails that winter on British shores have grey and brown streaked upper-parts and paler grey under-parts, long legs and a long, slightly upcurved bill twice the length of head.

Great Skua
Stercorarius skua

Great Skua

Size and Field Characteristics 54-58 cm.
Size of Herring Gull. A large, powerful, dark-brown-plumaged bird which shows white wing-patches in flight. Stout, black, hooked beak.
Status
Summer resident, oceanic in winter.
Habitat and Range
Breeds in Shetlands and north of Scotland. Winters in mid-Atlantic, and can be seen around British coasts during migration.
Nest
A large depression on ground among grass or heather, lined with heather, grass and moss.
Eggs
Olive-green with brown and grey markings. Clutch 1-2.
Food
Great Skuas harass other seabirds to the extent that they drop their catch of fish, which is then retrieved by the Skua. During breeding season young Kittiwakes are snatched from nests.

Arctic Skua
Stercorarius parasiticus

Arctic Skua

Size and Field Characteristics   42-46 cm.
Smaller than Herring Gull. 'Dimorphic' – having two
distinct forms of the same species. Dark phase, uniform
brown with paler colouring to cheeks. Light phase, pure
white under-parts, nape and cheeks. In Scotland 75% of
population are dark-phase, numbers of light birds
increasing in proportion the further north their range.
Status
Summer resident, oceanic in winter.
Habitat and Range
Moorlands of Orkneys and Shetlands and north-western
Scotland. Winters off coast of South Africa. Seen
around British coasts during autumn migration.
Nest
Depression in grass or heather, lined with similar
materials.
Eggs
Olive-brown with brown and grey markings. Clutch 2.
Food
The piratical Arctic Skua harasses Terns and other sea
birds until their fish catch is discarded; it is then
retrieved by the Skua. Small birds, mammals and carrion
are also taken.

Lesser Black-backed Gull
Larus fuscus

Lesser Black-backed Gull

Size and Field Characteristics 54 cm.
Smaller than Herring Gull. Dark-grey back and upper
wings with black outer feathers with white tips, head
and under-parts white, legs and beak yellow. In
breeding season beak has red spot near tip.

Status
Resident, with some birds moving south for winter.

Habitat and Range
Breeding Lesser Black-backs favour the coasts of north-
east Britain and Wales. Widespread during migration,
with large numbers wintering in the Midlands.
Scandinavian birds, which are slightly darker, also winter
in Britain.

Nest
On ground among vegetation built with weeds and
grasses.

Eggs
Olive, with blackish-brown and grey markings. Clutch 3.

Food
Largely fish, but omnivorous.

Great Black-backed Gull
Larus marinus

Great Black-backed Gull

Size and Field Characteristics 64-79 cm.
Larger than Herring Gull. Great Black-backed Gulls
have black wings and backs, white under-parts and
pinkish legs. Stout, powerful, slightly hooked yellow
beak with red spot.

Status
Resident.

Habitat and Range
Mainly rocky coasts and shoreline, but also inland
reservoirs, rubbish tips and river courses. Widespread
throughout the British Isles.

Nest
Usually situated on clifftops, built with grasses and other
vegetation.

Eggs
Stone-coloured, blotched and spotted with grey and
brown. Clutch 2-3.

Food
Fish, carrion, smaller sea-birds their eggs and young.
Also scavenges at rubbish tips.

Related Species
The Glaucous Gull (*Larus hyperboreus*) is similar in size
to the Great Black-backed Gull, recognized by its pearl-
grey wings and back with white under-parts. Glaucous
Gulls are winter visitors to southern Britain, but in the
north of Scotland a few can be seen throughout the
summer in and around fishing harbours.

Herring Gull
Larus argentatus

Herring Gull

Size and Field Characteristics   60 cm.
Most familiar Gull. Back and upper wings grey with
white spots on black tips, head and under-parts white,
pinkish legs, powerful yellow beak with red spot in
summer.
Status
Resident.
Habitat and Range
Widespread throughout Britain, favours coasts and islands
for breeding, some move inland in winter. Scandinavian
birds also winter in British Isles.
Nest
Bulky, built with seaweed and grasses usually in coastal
rocky situation.
Eggs
Olive-grey with dark-brown and grey markings.
Clutch 1-30.
Food
Fish, offal, scavenges at rubbish tips for scraps.
Related Species
The Iceland Gull (*Larus glaucoides*), 52 cm, is slightly
smaller than Herring Gull. Pale grey back and wings with
white tips, white head and under-parts, pinkish legs and
yellow beak. In winter, head slightly streaked. Small
numbers of Iceland Gulls from Greenland visit parts of the
British coast, and odd inland reservoirs, where they spend
the winter in the company of Herring Gulls. (Iceland
Gull).

Kittiwake
Rissa tridactyla

Kittiwake

Size and Field Characteristics 41 cm.
Smaller than Herring Gull. Grey back and wings with
jet-black wing-tips, head and under-parts white, black
legs and yellow beak. The Kittiwake is named after its
distinctive call.

Status
Resident, winters at sea.

Habitat and Range
Sea cliffs and islands around the British coast are the
breeding habitat of the Kittiwake. Few birds winter
around Britain's coasts, most winter off west coast of
Greenland.

Nest
Built on ledges on sea cliffs, also window ledges of high
buildings on harbourside. Substantially constructed with
grass and mud on seaweed base.

Eggs
Pale buff, spotted with dark-brown and grey and
blackish markings. Clutch 1-3.

Food
Feeds on fish, fish offal from fishing boats, and few
crustaceans. Unlike other Gulls it does not scavenge at
rubbish tips.

Sandwich Tern
Sterna sandvicensis

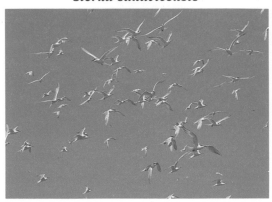

Sandwich Tern

Size and Field Characteristics   40 cm.
Larger than Black-headed Gull. Largest of British Terns.
Pale grey upper-parts, long narrow wings and deeply
forked tail, throat and under-parts white. Black cap with
shaggy crest, short black legs, yellow-tipped black bill is
about same length as head. Forehead is speckled white
in winter.

Status
Summer resident.

Habitat and Range
A bird of the coastal lagoons, sand dunes and grass-
covered islands. Nests in colonies, at times amid a
colony of Black-headed Gulls for protection. Like all
Terns, very unpredictable and easily disturbed while
nesting.

Nest
A scrape in the sand or scant vegetation.

Eggs
Pale buff, blotched with brown. Clutch l-2.

Food
Small fish, such as sprats and sandeels, which the
Sandwich Tern plunges under the surface to secure.

Little Tern
Sterna albifrons

Little Tern

Size and Field Characteristics   24 cm.
Smaller than Black-headed Gull. Smallest of the coastal
Terns. Upper-parts pearl-grey, underparts white, black
head with white heart-shaped mark on forehead, short
orange-yellow legs, and yellow bill with black tip.
Status
Summer resident.
Habitat and Range
Sandy and shingly coasts and estuaries around most of
British Isles except far north-west of Scotland. Winters
on West African coast.
Nest
A scrape in the sand or shingle, prone to disturbance by
humans on beaches. Occasionally contents destroyed by
unusually high tides or stormy weather.
Eggs
Pale buff to brown with darker blotches. Clutch 2-3.
Food
Small fish and sandeels, for which the Little Tern dives
close to the shore, hovering momentarily before diving.

Common Tern
Sterna hirundo

Common Tern

Size and Field Characteristics   34 cm.
Smaller than Black-headed Gull. Long, narrow, pointed wings and forked tail. Back and upperwings pearl-grey, with dark outer primary feathers, white under-parts, short red legs, black cap, red bill has black tip.
Status
Summer resident.
Habitat and Range
Found inland more than other Terns, where it nests on shingly gravel pits and along river courses. Also nests on coasts and islands. Widespread during migration but favours eastern side of country for breeding. Winters off West African coast.
Nest
Scrape in shingle or sand, colonial nester.
Eggs
Pale buff to brown with darker markings. Clutch 3.
Food
Small fish, marine crustaceans and water insects, which the Common Tern dives headlong into the water to secure.

Arctic Tern
Sterna paradisaea

Arctic Tern

Size and Field Characteristics 34 cm.
Similar in size to Common Tern, with which it may be
confused. In autumn, mixed flocks of juvenile Arctic
and Common Terns migrate together, referred to as
'Commic Terns'. Adult Arctic Tern lacks dark outer
primaries, and bill is completely red.

Status
Summer resident.

Habitat and Range
Small coastal islands and shingle banks. Favours the
north-eastern coastline for breeding. Less likely to breed
inland than Common Tern. Breeds in high northern
latitudes, then flies south to spend another summer just
north of Antarctic pack ice, making it our longest-
distance migratory bird.

Nest
Scrape in sand, shingle or turf.

Eggs
Greyish to brown with darker markings. Clutch 2-3.

Food
Small fish, sandeels and tiny crustaceans, taken from
below the surface by diving, often from hovering
position.

Roseate Tern
Sterna dougallii

Roseate Tern

Size and Field Characteristics 38 cm.
Larger than Common Tern. Whiter appearance than
both Common, and Arctic Terns, with paler back and
under-parts. Black cap, reddish legs, long tail-streamers
project well beyond wing tips when perched. In
breeding season breast has a rosy-pink tinge, and black
bill has reddish base.

Status
Summer resident.

Habitat and Range
Coastal estuaries and small islands. Can be seen round
most of British coastline during migration, but breeding
areas more restricted. Winters on West African shores.

Nest
Slight hollow on rock or sand, sometimes lined with a
few wispy pieces of vegetation.

Eggs
Creamy-buff, with darker markings. Clutch l-2.

Food
Small fish, sandeels.

Related Species
The Black Tern (*Chlidonias niger*), 24 cm, is seen in
Britain as a passage migrant in spring and autumn.
Black head and breast, grey wings and white undertail,
dark red legs and black bill. In autumn, the crown
remains black but neck and body are white, with white
collar.

Black Guillemot
Cepphus grylle

Black Guillemot

Size and Field Characteristics 34 cm.
Smaller than Wood Pigeon. Member of the Auk family.
Flies fast and low over water. In summer, striking black
plumage with large white wing patches, red legs and
pointed black beak. In winter, plumage very different,
head, neck and under-parts white with black markings,
back barred with black and white.

Status
Resident, winters at sea.

Habitat and Range
Rocky sea-coasts with boulder scree. Favours the north
and western coasts of Scotland as breeding habitat.
Some birds winter near breeding coasts, others move
south, becoming more oceanic.

Nest
A dark crevice among rocky scree or under large
boulder quite near water's edge, very little if any lining
added. Least colonial of Auks.

Eggs
Pale buff to greenish, blotched and spotted with
purplish-grey. Clutch 2.

Food
Fish, molluscs and crustaceans taken during dives of up
to sixty seconds in shallower inshore waters.

Little Auk
Alle alle

Little Auk

Size and Field Characteristics   21 cm.
Size of Starling, but different build, being a dumpy little
bird with large head and short neck. In summer, upper-
parts, head and breast black, under-parts white. Black,
stubby bill and dark grey legs with webbed feet. In
winter the lower half of the face and chin is off-white.
Greyish breast band.

Status
Mainly winter visitor. Non-breeder in British Isles.

Habitat and Range
A bird of the high Arctic Regions, seen mainly on eastern
shores of British Isles during or after stormy weather,
occasionally turns up inland.

Food
Feeds on zooplankton on or near the surface of the
water.

Guillemot
Uria aalge

Guillemot

Size and Field Characteristics 42 cm.
Larger than Pigeon. Member of the Auk family. Upright
Penguin-like stance on land, flies with rapid wingbeats.
Dark brown upper-parts and throat, white under-parts,
black pointed bill, some birds have white-spectacled
appearance. Known as 'Bridled Guillemots', this variety
is increasing percentage-wise, in the further north of
their range. In winter, most of face and throat white.

Status
Resident.

Habitat and Range
An oceanic species which comes ashore to nest
colonially on rocky ledges and tops of sea cliffs and
islands around the British Isles.

Nest
Huge numbers of Guillemots lay their single eggs on
bare, rocky ledges, in such crowded conditions that each
bird is within touching distance of a number of
neighbours.

Eggs
Variable, from off-white to buff and greenish-blue,
spotted and scribbled with black. Distinct pear shape
enables the egg to roll in a tight circle, thus lessening the
likelihood of it rolling over the edge. Clutch l.

Food
Fish, which the Guillemot can dive to a depth of over
45 m to secure.

Razorbill
Alca torda

Razorbill

Size and Field Characteristics   38 cm.
Slightly smaller than Pigeon. Upright Penguin-like
stance on land. More thick-set body than other
members of the Auk family. Black head, throat and
upper-parts. Curiously deep-shaped, black beak is
encircled by thin white line. In winter, white throat,
chin and cheeks.

Status
Resident, winters at sea.

Habitat and Range
An oceanic species which comes ashore to nest on sea
cliffs and rocky stacks around British coasts. Largest
colonies situated in Scotland and north of England.
Wintering birds can be seen in Bay of Biscay and
Mediterranean.

Nest
No nest as such, egg being laid on bare rocky ledge, in
crevice or under large boulder.

Eggs
Off-white, with brown and black markings. Clutch l.

Food
Fish, secured under surface by Razorbill propelling itself
with strong webbed feet and half-closed wings.

Puffin
Fratercula arctica

Puffin

Size and Field Characteristics 30 cm.
Smaller than Pigeon. Upright Penguin-like stance on
land. In summer black upper-parts, wings and upper tail,
white face and under-parts, short red legs and feet,
characteristic deep red, yellow and blue bill, red rim
round eyes. In winter, face is dark grey, bill is less
deep, dingy-orange at the tip and blackish at the base.
Status
Resident, winters at sea.
Habitat and Range
The grassy upper slopes of sea cliffs and islands and the
open sea. Largest colonies in northern Scotland, with
notable colonies in south and east England and Wales.
Nest
Usually in burrow or rabbit hole, one to two metres from
entrance, lined with grass and weeds.
Eggs
White, with occasional pale grey markings. Clutch l.
Food
Small fish such as sandeels. The Puffin is capable of
catching and holding half-a-dozen or so crosswise in its
peculiar bill, pursuing them in depths of up to fifteen
metres.

Rock Pipit
Anthus petrosus

Rock Pipit

Size and Field Characteristics 16.5 cm.
Slightly larger than Chaffinch. Upper-parts greyish-brown, pale breast with darker grey streaks. Slightly more robust than both Meadow and Tree Pipits, with grey, not white, outer tail feathers. Has similar display flight in breeding season, but from rock base.
Status
Resident.
Habitat and Range
In breeding season, rocky coasts and islands, in winter, mudflats, sandy shores and estuaries around British coastline.
Nest
Built with grasses, bents and hair, located under rocky boulder or in a crevice.
Eggs
Whitish flecked with greyish-brown. Clutch 4-5.
Food
Small marine crustaceans, insects and seeds.
Related Species
The Water Pipit (*Anthus spinoletta*), l7 cm, appears in south-eastern England as a winter visitor, in appearance is much paler than the three British breeding Pipits. The plumage is pale brown on the upper-parts, white eye-stripe, chin, throat and belly with a few greyish streaks on breast. Shy and difficult to observe.

Chough
Pyrrhocorax pyrrhocorax

Chough

Size and Field Characteristics 39 cm.
Larger than Jackdaw. Rarest of British Crows. Black
plumage, red legs and red downcurved bill about length
of head. Performs aerobatics in updraught above sea-
cliff habitat.
Status
Rare resident.
Habitat and Range
Confined to parts of the west coasts of Wales and
Scotland, where they frequent sea caves and cliffs.
Nest
Built on a rocky ledge in a sea cave or crevice in sea
cliff, constructed with sticks, twigs and wool.
Eggs
Pale blue, with markings of grey and brown. Clutch 3-6.
Food
Insects, spiders, seeds and plants.

Birds of Meadow, Moor and Mountain

Low-lying fields and damp meadows are a breeding habitat for a number of species, including Lapwing, Redshank and Skylark. In winter, such areas support thousands of Geese and other wildfowl that arrive in Britain from northern and eastern Europe.

Heather-covered Grouse moors and the more specialised peaty moorland of northern Scotland not only provide a habitat for the Red Grouse, but also a long and impressive list of birds, including Dunlin, Golden Plovers, Greenshank, Short-eared Owl and Hen Harrier.

Although many species found in the lower fields and meadows may also frequent hill moor country, the birds of the mountains are more specialised, choosing to live and breed among the high tops, such birds as the Ptarmigan, Snow Bunting and Golden Eagle.

Barnacle Goose
Branta leucopsis

Barnacle Goose

Size and Field Characteristics 60-70 cm.
Smaller than the Canada Goose. The Barnacle Goose is
an attractive little goose with a black neck and chest
contrasting with a white face and light under-parts. The
wings and back are barred with black, white and bluish-
grey. The short beak and longish legs are black.
Status
Winter visitor.
Habitat and Range
Barnacles frequent fields, marshes and estuaries in large
numbers. The Greenland breeding population of over
20,000 birds winters on the west coast of Scotland,
particularly on the island of Islay, whereas the breeding
population from Spitzbergen, numbering over 12,000
birds, winters on the Solway Firth in and around the
Wildfowl and Wetlands Reserve at Eastpark Farm.
Smaller numbers from the USSR can be seen at various
places on the east coast as far south as Kent.
Food
Mainly grasses.

White-fronted Goose
Anser albifrons

White-fronted Goose

Size and Field Characteristics   65-70 cm.
Smaller than the Canada Goose. A grey Goose with
black blotches on its breast, a white rump and orange
legs. Distinctive white patch at base of bill. Two
different races winter in the British Isles, European
White-fronts have pinkish bills. Greenland White-fronts
have orange bills.

Status
Winter visitor.

Habitat and Range
Fields and meadows near rivers, estuaries and other
expanses of water. European White-fronts from the
USSR winter around the Severn estuary. Greenland
White-fronts can be found wintering in Scotland, mainly
on west coast, and northern parts of Ireland.

Food
Mainly grasses.

Lesser White-fronted Goose
Anser erythropus

Lesser White-fronted Goose

Size and Field Characteristics 50-65 cm.
Slightly smaller than other White-fronts, the Lesser
White-front is a rare visitor to the British Isles. It is
distinguished from other White-fronts by having a larger
patch of white at the base of the bill, and distinctive
yellow rims round its eyes, the black barring on its
breast is less noticeable.

Status
Rare winter visitor.

Habitat and Range
Only one or two birds turn up annually on the Severn
estuary near Slimbridge, where they mingle with
European White-fronts. The breeding range of the
Lesser White-front is northern Europe.

Food
Mainly grasses.

Pink-footed Goose
Anser brachyrhynchus

Pink-footed Goose

Size and Field Characteristics 60-75 cm.
Smaller than Canada Goose. The Pink-foot is the
smallest grey Goose regularly seen in Britain. Besides
having the typical greyish-brown barring of the grey
Geese on its wings and back, the legs are pink. The
beak has a black base and tip, hence it looks dark from
a distance.
Status
Winter visitor.
Habitat and Range
In late September Pink-feet arrive from Iceland and
Greenland. They frequent estuaries, mud flats and
fields, and are more likely to be seen among root crops
than any other grey geese. Many thousands of Pink-feet
winter in central Scotland, the Solway Firth and areas on
the east and west coasts of England.
Food
Grass, grain and root crops.

Greylag Goose
Anser anser

Greylag Goose

Size and Field Characteristics   75-90 cm.
Smaller than Canada Goose. A grey Goose with
typically barred greyish-brown back and wings. Pale
head and neck, distinct orange bill and pink legs.
Status
Some resident pairs, but mainly winter visitors.
Habitat and Range
In winter, Greylags from Iceland frequent arable fields,
marshes and lochs. Feral pairs breed in a number of
locations throughout the British Isles, with truly wild
birds breeding in parts of the west and north of
Scotland.
Nest
On ground, usually constructed with and among reeds.
As incubation progresses, down is added.
Eggs
Creamy-white. Clutch 4-6.
Food
Grass, grain, potatoes and cereal shoots.
Related Species
The Bean Goose (*Anser fabalis*), 65-80 cm, is a grey
Goose with orange legs. Its bill has a black base and
tip. The Bean Goose is a scarce winter visitor to parts of
south-east England, south-west Scotland and the Moray
Firth area, where it feeds in grass fields.

Marsh Harrier
Circus aeruginosus

Marsh Harrier

Size and Field Characteristics   48-56 cm.
Similar size to Buzzard. Largest of the Harriers. The
male has dark-brown body, yellowish head, brown and
grey wings with black tips, grey tail. The female has
dark-brown body with yellowish head and forewings.
Like other Harriers the Marsh Harrier flies low over open
ground.
Status
Mainly summer visitor with a few breeding pairs.
Habitat and Range
The reed beds of East Anglia are the main breeding
haunts of Marsh Harriers in this country.
Nest
A bulky, reedy platform built among tall reeds.
Eggs
Bluish-white. Clutch 3-5.
Food
Small mammals, birds and frogs. In breeding season
spectacular mid-air food pass from male to female.
Related Species
The Montagu's Harrier (*Circus pygargus*), at 40-45 cm, is
the smallest Harrier, and a summer resident. Found
breeding in small numbers in south-eastern England.
The male is predominantly grey with black wing-tips and
a thin black line along the upper wings. The female is
brown, with dark and light-brown barring on her tail.
White rump.

Hen Harrier
Circus cyaneus

Hen Harrier

Size and Field Characteristics 45-52 cm.
Smaller than Buzzard. The male is light grey, with white
under-parts and rump, and black wing-tips. The female
is larger, brownish-coloured with white rump, and light
and dark brown barred tail.
Status
Resident.
Habitat and Range
Rough heather moorland and young conifer plantations
in north of England and over wider areas of Scotland,
are the breeding haunts of the Hen Harrier. In winter
marshes and farmland near the coast.
Nest
A depression on the ground lined with heather stalks
and grasses.
Eggs
Bluish-white. Clutch 3-6.
Food
Small mammals and birds. In breeding season
spectacular mid-air food pass from male to female.

Golden Eagle
Aquila chrysaetos

Golden Eagle

Size and Field Characteristics   75-85 cm.
Much larger than Buzzard. A very large raptor with a
wingspan of over two metres. Dark-brown in colour
with golden-yellow head and neck and noticeably large
powerful beak. In flight wings are held in a shallow 'V'.
Immature birds have white patches on wings and tail.

Status
Resident.

Habitat and Range
Wild mountainous country of the Scottish Highlands,
particularly the west. Also Galloway Hills, the Lake
District and occasionally hills of southern Scotland.

Nest
On remote rocky ledge or pine tree, the birds usually
having two or three alternative sites which become very
bulky constructions of sticks, branches, bracken and
heather, over many years.

Eggs
Whitish with varying degrees of brownish-grey markings.
Clutch 1-2.

Food
Mountain hares, rabbits, grouse and other birds, carrion.

Related Species
The White-tailed Eagle (*Haliaeetus albicilla*) has a
wingspan of almost three metres, a paler head and more
massive beak than the Golden Eagle, and the tail in
mature birds is white.

Kestrel
Falco tinnunculus

Kestrel

Size and Field Characteristics 34-38 cm.
Smaller than Pigeon. The most familiar bird of prey.
Male has chestnut upper-parts with black spots. Bluish-grey head and tail with black band near the tip. Pointed wings. Female has chestnut upper-parts with brown barring on the back, and brown-streaked head and breast. Unlike all our other birds of prey the sexes are similar in size.
Status
Resident.
Habitat and Range
Kestrels can be seen hovering over open ground, moorland, parkland, motorway verges and urban parks.
Widespread throughout the British Isles.
Nest
Does not build a nest as such, lays its eggs in scrape on cliff ledge, hole in tree or old nest of other bird. A variety of sites, including window ledges in urban habitat.
Eggs
White with reddish-brown markings. Clutch 3-6.
Food
Small mammals, small birds, beetles, stalked from some vantage point or while hovering.

Merlin
Falco columbarius

Merlin

Size and Field Characteristics   27-32 cm.
Smaller than Kestrel. The male Merlin, only the size of a
Mistle Thrush, is our smallest Falcon. He has bluish
upper-parts, dark grey barring on his tail, and reddish
breast streaked with brown. Faint moustachial stripe.
The female has brownish upper-parts, a paler breast
streaked with brown and light and dark brown barred
tail.
Status
Resident.
Habitat and Range
In summer, heather moorland of Scotland, north of
England and Wales. In winter, follows Pipits to coastal
areas.
Nest
Usually a scrape on ground among heather, but in some
areas prefers to nest in old crow nests.
Eggs
Whitish, blotched with reddish-brown. Clutch 3-6.
Food
Small birds, small mammals, insects. Birds usually taken
following fast and, at times, lengthy chase.

Peregrine
Falco peregrinus

Peregrine

Size and Field Characteristics 36-48 cm.
Larger than Pigeon. A most impressive, powerful
Falcon. The male has slate-grey upper-parts and tail
which is noticeably shorter than those of broad-winged
raptors such as Sparrow Hawk. He has dark-grey head
and moustachial stripe, which contrasts with white chin.
Under-parts are whitish barred with black. Female is
noticeably larger and slightly duller. Both sexes have
long pointed wings.
Status
Resident.
Habitat and Range
Mountainous country and hilly regions of Scotland,
Wales and parts of the west of England are the summer
haunts of the Peregrine. In winter, estuaries are
frequented.
Nest
A scrape on cliff ledge, no material added, but often
uses old Raven nest where available.
Eggs
Whitish, blotched with deep reddish-brown. Clutch 3-4.
Food
Mainly Dove-sized birds, taken after spectacular 'stoop',
when Peregrine can dive, at over 150 miles per hour,
from aerial vantage point. Birds smaller and larger than
Doves are also taken, also a few mammals.

Snowy Owl
Nyctea scandiaca

Snowy Owl

Size and Field Characteristics 53-60 cm.
Slightly larger than Buzzard. Can be seen hunting
during daylight hours, when flight resembles that of
Buzzard. The male is almost pure white, with striking
yellow eyes, the plumage of the female is barred in
dark-grey and white. Feet feathered to the toes.
Status
Rare resident, more often seen as winter visitor.
Habitat and Range
Rough open tundra-like ground. Has bred on Fetlar in
the Shetlands. Arrives in far north of Scotland for winter
from Arctic regions.
Nest
A scrape on small hillock, sometimes scantily lined with
grass or moss.
Eggs
White. Clutch 4-8.
Food
Hares, rodents and birds.

Red Grouse
Lagopus lagopus

Red Grouse

Size and Field Characteristics 38-42 cm.
About Pigeon size with much rounder body. Both male and female are mottled reddish-brown, with a few white bars on the flanks, and greyish-white feathering down to and including the toes. Males have distinct red wattles.

Status
Resident.

Habitat and Range
The open heather-covered moors of Scotland, Wales, Ireland and northern England are the breeding haunts of the Red Grouse, particularly controlled Grouse moors, where the characteristic call 'go-back go-back go-back' is uttered by the territorial cocks.

Nest
A mere scrape well hidden among heather.

Eggs
Off-white, blotched with dark brown. Clutch 7-10.

Food
Heather shoots, seeds and berries.

Ptarmigan
Lagopus mutus

Ptarmigan

Size and Field Characteristics   35 cm.
Slightly smaller than Red Grouse but similar shape.
Three distinct plumage changes throughout year.
Feathered to their toes, Ptarmigans in winter are pure
white, with black tails, the male has black eye-stripe. In
summer, the male is mottled in shades of brown and
grey with white under-parts, black tail and red wattles,
while the female is mottled in lighter shades. In autumn,
the male is mottled in lighter shades of brown and grey
and the female turns darker.
Status
Resident.
Habitat and Range
The Scottish mountains, seldom seen below 700 metres.
Nest
A scrape on lichen-covered rocks or among stunted
heather.
Eggs
Creamy with dark brown blotches. Clutch 6-9.
Food
Heather shoots, seeds and other plants.

Black Grouse
Tetrao tetrix

Black Grouse

Size and Field Characteristics   40-55 cm.
Larger than Red Grouse. The female Black Grouse, or
'Greyhen', is slightly larger and greyer-plumaged than
the Red Grouse. The male Black Grouse, or 'Blackcock',
is much larger than the female and is unmistakable in his
glossy-black plumage with white wing markings, and
lyre-shaped tail, under which the pure white feathers are
noticeable during the 'lek', the communal spring display,
when the males show off to each other, early in the
morning or late evening.
Status
Resident.
Habitat and Range
Moorland edges bordering conifer plantations, large
expanses of grass, and bracken-covered hills. The hilly,
moorland areas of Scotland, Wales and the north of
Scotland.
Nest
A well-concealed depression on ground among long
grass or bracken.
Eggs
Creamy, spotted with reddish-brown. Clutch 5-8.
Food
Pine and larch buds, blaeberries and moorland plants.

Pheasant
Phasianus colchicus

Pheasant

Size and Field Characteristics Male 75 cm, female 60 cm, including long tail.
The Pheasant is a well-known bird of the British countryside. The male's brilliant plumage is bronze, purple, chestnut and green, some birds having distinct white collar. The female is brown, mottled in a darker shade, necessary for concealment while incubating.
Status
Resident.
Habitat and Range
Woodlands and farmlands with patches of good undergrowth cover, copses and hedgerows. Widespread throughout the British Isles except for the north-western corner of Scotland.
Nest
A leaf-lined scrape among dense vegetation, such as bramble or bracken.
Eggs
Shades of olive. Clutch l0-20.
Food
Seeds, grains, worms, plants, berries and insects.

Quail
Coturnix coturnix

Quail

Size and Field Characteristics 17 cm.
Shorter than Starling and much dumpier, with very short
tail. Very difficult to observe because of secretive habits.
Both sexes have pale brown upper-parts with darker
streaks and whitish eye-stripe. The male has dark-
brown streaks on the throat. Characteristic triple
whistling call usually the only indication that Quail are
present.
Status
Summer resident, the only game bird in this category.
Habitat and Range
Mainly a bird of the cereal fields of the south of England,
also found frequenting barley fields in southern
Scotland. Winters in Central and South Africa.
Nest
A scantily-lined scrape on ground among vegetation.
Eggs
Yellowish-brown, blotched with dark brown.
Clutch 7-12.
Food
Plant shoots and seeds, insects.

Red-legged Partridge
Alectoris rufa

Red-legged Partridge

Size and Field Characteristics   34 cm.
Both sexes have chestnut-brown upper-parts with
orange and grey under-parts. The flanks are barred with
black, white and chestnut. White face with black eye-
stripe. Beak and legs blood-red. Often perches on post
or wall, and less likely to take flight than Grey Partridge.
Status
Resident.
Habitat and Range
Arable land and open country over most of England, the
eastern half of Wales and southern and eastern Scotland.
Nest
A grass-lined scrape on ground among vegetation.
Eggs
Creamy, spotted with brown. Clutch l0-l4.
Food
Plant shoots, seeds, slugs and insects.

Grey Partridge
Perdix perdix

Grey Partridge

Size and Field Characteristics 30 cm.
Smaller than Pigeon. The Grey Partridge has a plump, round body, brownish-grey on the back, thin whitish streaks on the wings and grey under-parts with chestnut barred flanks. Male has distinct horseshoe mark on lower breast, less distinct in female.

Status
Resident.

Habitat and Range
The traditional mixed farms with hedgerow cover and uncultivated field edges are the haunts of the Grey Partridge. Widespread, except for far north-west of Scotland, but scarce in many areas due to modern farming methods.

Nest
A scrape concealed in undergrowth, lined with grass and leaves.

Eggs
Glossy, pale-brown. Clutch 8-16.

Food
Seeds, leaves and grain. Newly-hatched chicks are dependent on insects which are pests on farmland.

Corncrake
Crex crex

Corncrake

Size and Field Characteristics   28 cm.
Smaller than Moorhen. The Corncrake is a chicken-like
bird, with brown and black mottled upper-parts, greyish
head and chestnut coloured wings. Characteristic 'crek-
crek' call.
Status
Summer resident.
Habitat and Range
Hayfields and rough pasture. Once widespread, now
confined to the north-west of Scotland, the Western Isles
and the west of Ireland, where older forms of farming,
such as haymaking, are still practiced. Winters in Central
Africa.
Nest
Grass-lined depression in grass tussock.
Eggs
Creamy-coloured, blotched with brown. Clutch 6-l0.
Food
Worms, insects and seeds.

Avocet
Recurvirostra avosetta

Avocet

Size and Field Characteristics 44 cm.
Larger than Lapwing. A black and white wader with long blue-grey legs. Slim slightly upturned bill about twice length of head.
Status
Resident.
Habitat and Range
Muddy coastal lagoons of East Anglia are the main breeding haunts of the Avocet. In winter they move to the estuaries of south as well as eastern England.
Nest
A slight scrape with scanty lining, on small, low-lying island.
Eggs
Buffish, spotted with dark-brown. Clutch 3-4.
Food
Small shrimps and insect larvae, which the Avocet sweeps its bill from side to side through the water to extract.

Stone Curlew
Burhinus oedicnemus

Stone Curlew

Size and Field Characteristics   42 cm.
Larger than Lapwing. The Stone Curlew is sandy-brown
with dark-brown streaks on the upper parts.
Conspicuous black and white wing pattern in flight.
Thick yellow legs, large yellow eyes and yellow bill
shorter than length of head.
Status
Rare summer resident.
Habitat and Range
Sandy heaths and chalk downs of south-eastern England
are the summer haunts of the Stone Curlew. In winter,
birds move to southern Europe and Africa. Occasionally
a few birds winter on south coast.
Nest
A scrape in the bare soil.
Eggs
Pale buff, blotched and marked with brown. Clutch 2.
Food
Molluscs, earthworms, beetles and other insects, stalked
mainly during the night.

Dotterel
Charadrius morinellus

Dotterel

Size and Field Characteristics 22 cm.
Smaller than Lapwing. Colourful little wader with
greyish brown mantle and breast, chestnut belly, white
breast-band and undertail coverts. White eye-stripes
which meet at back of head. Female slightly more
colourful than male. Short yellowish legs, short bill less
than length of head, winter plumage slightly duller.
Status
Summer resident.
Habitat and Range
Found among stunted heather on Scotland's hills and
mountains, usually above 840 metres. Can be seen in
lower regions during spring migration. Winters in North
Africa.
Nest
A scrape among stunted heather.
Eggs
Buffish, heavily marked with black. Clutch 3.
Food
Beetles, flying and other insects.

Golden Plover
Pluvialis apricaria

Golden Plover

Size and Field Characteristics 28 cm.
Smaller than Lapwing. Golden-yellow spangled upper-
parts, black chin, throat and belly with whitish border.
Short bill, less than the length of roundish head. In
winter, breast is mottled and belly white.

Status
Resident and winter visitor.

Habitat and Range
Sparsely-covered heathery hills and high moorland are
the summer haunts of the Golden Plover. In winter,
estuaries and coastal farmland support many thousands
when numbers are increased with Scandinavian and
Icelandic birds. Widespread throughout the British Isles,
breeds in Scotland, north of England and central Wales.

Nest
A scantily-lined scrape among short vegetation.

Eggs
Yellowish-buff, blotched by blackish-brown. Clutch 3-4.

Food
Insects and seeds.

Related Species
The Grey Plover (*Pluvialis squatarola*) is similarly
shaped and sized. A winter visitor to British shores and
estuaries from USSR, the Grey Plover is then spangled
light and dark grey above, with paler under-parts and
black legs. In summer, face, throat and belly are jet-
black with white borders.

Lapwing
Vanellus vanellus

Lapwing

Size and Field Characteristics 30 cm.
Smaller than Pigeon. A familiar wader. At a distance
looks black and white, but upper-parts are dark glossy-
green with purplish highlights. Black breast, white belly,
orange undertail, wispy black crest, beak shorter than
length of head. Characteristic 'peewit' call in territory.
Status
Resident.
Habitat and Range
In summer, cultivated ground, moorland and damp
meadows. In winter, fields by coast and estuaries.
Widespread throughout the British Isles.
Nest
A scrape on ground, lined to varying degrees with bits of
straw or reeds.
Eggs
Buffish, heavily marked with black blotches. Clutch 4.
Food
Earthworms, slugs, snails, insects.

Snipe
Gallinago gallinago

Snipe

Size and Field Characteristics   26 cm.
Larger than Ringed Plover. Light and dark streaked
upper-parts, brown mottled breast and undertail, white
belly, longish green legs and long bill fully twice length
of brown streaked head. In breeding territory, while
performing steep diving display, a characteristic
'drumming' sound is made by the male.

Status
Resident.

Habitat and Range
Boggy edges of lakes, ponds and other watery places,
marshes and water meadows. Widespread throughout
the British Isles.

Nest
A neat cup concealed in grass or reed tussock, built with
rushes and grasses.

Eggs
Background varies from olive to grey, blotched with
black markings. Clutch 4.

Food
Earthworms, insects, small crustaceans, for which Snipe
probe deep into the soft mud.

Jack Snipe
Lymnocryptes minimus

Jack Snipe

Size and Field Characteristics 19 cm.
Smaller than Common Snipe, noticeably streaked light
and dark brown upper-parts, double eye-stripe, brown
mottled under-parts, short legs and short bill about
length of head. Bobbing action when walking. When
disturbed, flies a short distance then lands again.

Status
Passage migrant, seen in British Isles in every month of
the year.

Habitat and Range
Expanses of marshy and boggy areas with soft muddy
edges and small open patches among reeds. Widely
distributed throughout England, Wales and the southern
half of Scotland, but scarce and elusive. Breeds in
northern Europe.

Food
Worms and other invertebrates, for which the Jack Snipe
probes into the mud.

Curlew
Numenius arquata

Curlew

Size and Field Characteristics 55 cm.
Largest British wader. Upper-parts patterned with
uniform streaks of brown; head, breast and under-parts
also streaked but paler, greenish legs and long
downcurved bill, over twice the length of head in some
females. Characteristic 'cur-loo' call in breeding territory.
Status
Resident and winter visitor.
Habitat and Range
Breeds on hill moors, farm meadows and reedy areas
throughout British Isles except for south-eastern
England. Winters on coast, some British birds moving
south when larger numbers arrive from Scandinavia.
Nest
Large scrape on ground, lined with fine grasses.
Eggs
Greenish to olive, spotted with grey and brown. Clutch
4.
Food
Earthworms, insects and larvae, molluscs and
crustaceans, which the Curlew probes into soft sand to
locate and secure with sensitive tip of long bill.

Whimbrel
Numenius phaeopus

Whimbrel

Size and Field Characteristics 40 cm.
Smaller than Curlew but similarly shaped. Upper-parts
patterned with uniform streaks of brown, paler brown
streaked head with black stripe above eyes, pale rump,
greenish-grey legs and long down-curved bill, twice the
length of head.

Status
Summer resident and passage migrant.

Habitat and Range
Main breeding population found in Shetland Isles, with
other northern areas supporting breeding birds. During
spring migration, birds en route to Scandinavian and
Icelandic breeding grounds can be seen on British
coasts, particularly on the southern and eastern sides of
the country.

Nest
Scrape on ground, lined with heather and grasses.

Eggs
Olive-brown with brown and greyish blothes.
Clutch 3-4.

Food
Worms, insects and their larvae, molluscs and berries.

Ruff
Philomachus pugnax

Ruff

Size and Field Characteristics   Male 30 cm, female 24 cm.

Larger than Ringed Plover. In breeding plumage, male Ruffs are extraordinary, each bird having a large ruff and head tuft, in a range of colours from white to purplish black, which are displayed at 'leks' to attract females. Females are noticeably smaller than males, with brown patterned upper-parts, lighter head and breast, white undertail, longish legs, slightly downcurved beak about length of head. In winter, upper-parts greyish, with whitish head and under-parts.

Status

Rare summer resident, mainly passage migrant and winter visitor.

Habitat and Range

A few pairs breed in wet meadows in East Anglia. In autumn, migrants from Scandinavia pass through British Isles en route to Africa, some birds staying to winter in such places as the Ouse Washes, also estuaries. Seen throughout British Isles except northern half of Scotland.

Nest

Scantily-lined depression in grass tussock.

Eggs

Olive, blotched with greyish-brown. Clutch 3-4.

Food

Worms, seeds, beetles and other insects.

Redshank
Tringa totanus

Redshank

Size and Field Characteristics   28 cm.
Smaller than Lapwing. Brown upper-parts with darker
spots, paler under-parts, white rear edge of wings
noticeable in flight, long red legs and straight beak about
length of head.

Status
Resident and winter visitor.

Habitat and Range
In summer, wet meadows and marshes over most of
British Isles. In winter, more widespread particularly
coastal. Some British birds move south when Icelandic
birds migrate to Britain for winter.

Nest
Well-concealed in reedy tussock, a neat cup of reeds
and fine grass.

Eggs
Yellowish-brown, blotched and spotted with reddish-
brown. Clutch 4.

Food
Earthworms, small crustaceans and molluscs.

Related Species
The Spotted Redshank (*Tringa erythropus*), at 30 cm, is
slightly larger than Redshank, has dark red legs, and
blackish plumage in summer, and differing from
Redshank in winter, with paler under-parts, greyer back
and longer bill. Spotted Redshank are passage migrants,
a few remain for winter, mainly in the south.

Greenshank
Tringa nebularia

Greenshank

Size and Field Characteristics 30 cm.
Larger than Redshank. Dark-grey upper-parts, lighter
grey head and breast with dark grey markings, white
belly and rump noticeable in flight, longish green legs
and slightly up-curved bill longer than length of head.

Status
Summer resident and passage migrant.

Habitat and Range
The open peat and heathery moors studded with
lochans in the north of Scotland support breeding pairs.
Most birds are seen during autumn migration, moving
from Scandinavian breeding grounds to winter quarters
in Africa.

Nest
Scrape on ground, lined with heather stalks and grasses,
usually close to object such as an old log.

Eggs
Pale yellowish-brown, blotched and spotted with rusty-
red. Clutch 4.

Food
Aquatic insects and their larvae, worms, small fish, which
Greenshank make erratic dashes through the shallow
water to secure.

Red-necked Phalarope
Phalaropus lobatus

Red-necked Phalarope

Size and Field Characteristics 18 cm.
Smaller than Starling. In summer boldly marked, brown
upper-parts, grey head, white throat, reddish-brown
neck, greenish legs and straight black bill slightly longer
than length of head. Female brighter than male. In
winter, upper-parts are greyish; white head with dark
grey crown and cheeks. Extremely tame, allowing close
approach without showing alarm.

Status
Scarce summer resident.

Habitat and Range
The heather moors, bogs and marshes dotted with small
lochans on the Shetland Islands are the summer haunts
of the Red-necked Phalarope. Odd birds en route to
their oceanic wintering grounds are occasionally seen on
the south-east coast of England.

Nest
Concealed in grassy tussock, lined with fine grasses, and
situated close to the water's edge.

Eggs
Olive-brown with chocolate-brown markings. Clutch 4.

Food
Insects and larvae picked from water, following
disturbance caused by Phalarope spinning around in
tight circles to bring food items to surface. During this
procedure, again shows no fear of man.

Black-headed Gull
Larus ridibundus

Black-headed Gull

Size and Field Characteristics   35 cm.
Only about half the size of Herring Gull. In summer, pearl-grey back and wings with black tips to primary feathers. Reddish legs and beak, distinct chocolate-brown head. In winter no brown head, only dark spots around and behind eyes.

Status
Resident.

Habitat and Range
Moorland with pools, marshes and estuaries.
Widespread throughout British Isles. Absent as breeding species from central and south-west England.

Nest
Depression among reeds or heather, lined with heather and grass, situated near water.

Eggs
Variable from pale olive to dark-brown with darker markings. Clutch 3.

Food
Fish, crustaceans, worms, scavenges at rubbish tips; in spring, follows the plough for worms and grubs.

Related Species
The Little Gull (*Larus minutus*), 26 cm, a scarce passage migrant, can turn up in any month of the year in juvenile plumage, with dark zig-zag pattern on upper wings, white head with dark crown and black spot on cheek. Adults have black heads in summer, greyish in winter.

Common Gull
Larus canus

Common Gull

Size and Field Characteristics 42 cm.
Smaller than Herring Gull, which it resembles at a
distance. Greyish wings with white spots on black wing-
tips, white head and under-parts, yellowish-green legs
and beak. In winter, head tinged with grey-brown.
Status
Resident.
Habitat and Range
Coastal and inland waters, arable and grass fields
throughout British Isles, breeds almost entirely in
Scotland.
Nest
A depression among vegetation, lined with seaweed on
coastal sites, and grass inland, where most colonies are
located.
Eggs
Olive-green, with dark brown markings. Clutch 3.
Food
Fish, worms, insects; scavenges for scraps at rubbish tips.
Related Species
The Mediterranean Gull (*Larus melanocephalus*), 36 cm,
is slightly smaller than Common Gull. In summer, has
black head, red beak, and no black on wing tips. In
winter, head almost pure white except for dusky marks
round eyes, and darker beak. A rare species found on
south-east coast in spring.

Nightjar
Caprimulgus europaeus

Nightjar

Size and Field Characteristics   28 cm.
Smaller than Kestrel. Crepuscular – active in twilight.
Upper-parts, wings and tail cunningly marked and
barred with shades of grey, brown and black, making
the female almost invisible on the ground. Male has
white spots near wing tips and on outer tips of tail,
perches lengthways on decaying branch, making him
similarly difficult to observe. Good identification feature
is characteristic 'churring' song heard after dark.

Status
Summer resident.

Habitat and Range
Bushy heaths and commons, and areas where conifers
have been felled, leaving brushwood ground cover.
Breeding distribution is patchy, but mainly in England.
Winters in Africa.

Nest
A scrape on the ground among undergrowth or decaying
brushwood.

Eggs
White blotched with brown and violet. Clutch 2.

Food
Nightjars are equipped with wide gapes, ideal for
catching their moth prey in the dark, which they catch
by twisting and turning in erratic fashion.

Short-eared Owl
Asio flammeus

Short-eared Owl

Size and Field Characteristics 38 cm.
Similar in size to Tawny Owl. Regularly seen hunting during daylight, when low flapping flight is good identification feature. Upper-parts mottled in shades of brown; buff and brown streaked breast, paler underneath; dark hooked beak and talons, yellow eyes. Short ear-tufts displayed when alarmed.

Status
Resident.

Habitat and Range
Rough or heathery ground and young conifer plantations are the breeding habitat of the Short-eared Owl. In winter they move south to lower-lying farmland and coastal areas with scrub cover and marshes.

Nest
A depression on the ground among heather or reeds, and in rough grass among young conifers.

Eggs
White. Clutch 3-11.

Food
Mostly short-tailed voles, other small mammals and birds.

Egg-laying Sequence of Hawks and Owls

Hawks, Falcons and Owls lay their eggs with an interval of two to three days between each egg. This leads to young birds of different ages occupying the same nest.

When examining a family of four young Kestrels when the oldest chick is fourteen days old, at first glance there will be little obvious difference in size or plumage, even though the oldest bird is about a week older than the youngest. The same family when seen fourteen days later, reveals a different situation, the now twenty-eight day old chick is almost ready to leave the nest, while the youngest is still quite downy, the remaining youngsters being at varying stages between the two.

In a good vole year a Short-eared Owl nest with ten eggs is not uncommon, again the eggs are laid at two-day intervals and hatch accordingly. By the time the last egg has hatched the first youngster's plumage is well developed, so much so that the youngster has shuffled a fair distance from the nest, and is lying concealed among tussocky grass; the other members of the family will do likewise in turn, but in different directions. This behaviour lessens the chances of the whole family being destroyed by a marauding fox or other predator, and the roving chicks are in constant contact with their parents. The differing sizes of the youngsters in these species also ensure survival of the fittest if there is a sudden drop in the availability of prey.

Skylark
Alauda arvensis

Skylark

Size and Field Characteristics 18 cm.
Smaller than Starling. Upper-parts mottled with shades
of light and dark brown, under-parts paler with a few
dark streaks on breast, white outer tail feathers, short
crest. Characteristic, clear warbling song as Skylark rises
and circles in the air above breeding territory is good
identification feature. Seen in flocks in winter.

Status
Resident.

Habitat and Range
Open fields, meadows, moors, pastures and golf courses
throughout the British Isles.

Nest
A hair-lined grassy cup, well concealed among low
vegetation.

Eggs
Greyish speckled with brown. Clutch 3-6.

Food
Grain, seeds, insects, worms and young leaves.

Related Species
The Shore Lark (*Eremophila alpestris*), 16.5 cm, slightly
smaller than Skylark. Scarce winter visitor to eastern
seaboard. Rare breeder on Scottish mountain tops.
Male strikingly coloured, brown back tinged and
streaked with pink, under-parts whitish, crown cheeks
and throat black, rest of head bright yellow, sports a pair
of black feathery 'horns'. Female less colourful.

Meadow Pipit
Anthus pratensis

Meadow Pipit

Size and Field Characteristics   14.5 cm.
Similar size to Chaffinch. Most numerous small bird
seen on moorland walk. Upper-parts olive-brown with
darker streaks, under-parts paler, also streaked with
brown. White outer tail feathers. Prefers to perch on
ground. During spring display rises into air almost
vertically, then parachutes down while singing, a good
identification feature.
Status
Resident.
Habitat and Range
Open ground, mostly upland moors in breeding season.
Move to lower coastal areas in winter, where they roam
in small flocks.
Nest
Built with grasses and bents and lined with finer
material, concealed in reeds, heather or grassy tussock
on ground.
Eggs
Finely mottled in greyish brown. Clutch 4-5.
Food
Insects, spiders, grasshoppers etc.

Cuckoo
Cuculus canorus

Cuckoo

Size and Field Characteristics 33 cm.
Smaller than Wood Pigeon. Resembles Sparrowhawk.
Grey upper-parts, breast and long tail, under-parts boldly
barred with dark-grey and white, white spots on tail,
short yellow legs and feet and dark bill. Perches with
wing-tips drooped below slightly cocked tail. The 'coo-
coo' call is a familiar sound in Cuckoo territory in spring.
Status
Summer resident.
Habitat and Range
Open woodland, moorland, farmland and reedy areas,
widespread throughout British Isles. Adults leave Britain
for African wintering grounds approximately four weeks
before young.
Nest
The Cuckoo builds no nest of its own, laying its eggs in
those of Meadow Pipit, Reed Warbler and Dunnock, as
well as a range of other small insect-eating birds.
Eggs
Closely resemble those of foster parent, though slightly
larger; the Cuckoo removes one egg from the nest with
its beak, before laying one of its own in the nest. As
many as a dozen eggs laid in a season, but only one in
each nest.
Food
Insects and invertebrates.

Whinchat
Saxicola rubetra

Whinchat

Size and Field Characteristics 13 cm.
Smaller than Chaffinch. Male upper-parts streaked in
shades of brown with white wing patches, black cheeks
bordered by white eye-stripes and semi-collars, breast
buffish, belly white. Female paler with less white in
plumage. Perches prominently on telegraph wires, wall,
post or topmost twig on low bush.
Status
Summer resident.
Habitat and Range
Open country with scrubby bushes, rough roadside
verges, young conifer plantations. Widespread
throughout the British Isles where habitat is suitable.
Winters in Africa.
Nest
Concealed in grass tussock on ground, built with grasses
and moss and lined with hair.
Eggs
Bluish-green, faintly marked with brown. Clutch 4-6.
Food
Insects and spiders, occasionally small worms.

Stonechat
Saxicola torquata

Stonechat

Size and Field Characteristics 12.5 cm.
Smaller than Chaffinch. In summer, the male has brown
and black streaked back, black head, white patches on
side of neck and an orange breast. Female plumage is
duller with buffish head. In winter, male closely
resembles female. The Stonechat is a plump little bird
and perches prominently on telegraph wires or bushes,
uttering characteristic 'chac-chac' call when alarmed.
Status
Resident.
Habitat and Range
Young conifer plantations, open country with gorse
particularly near coast. Mainly found breeding on
western side of Britain.
Nest
Concealed on ground among vegetation, built with grass
and moss, lined with hair.
Eggs
Greenish-blue, speckled with reddish-brown. Clutch 5-6.
Food
Insects and other small invertebrates.

Wheatear
Oenanthe oenanthe

Wheatear

Size and Field Characteristics 15 cm.
Length of Chaffinch but stockier. Male has blue-grey head and back, broad black eye-stripe, wings and tip of tail in shape of inverted 'T'; pale orange breast and white rump is good identification feature in both male and less colourful female. Wheatears flit restlessly from stone to stone, always perched in prominent position when settled.

Status
Summer resident.

Habitat and Range
Open country, particularly in upland areas with dry-stone walls and old tree stumps. Widespread throughout British Isles, but absent as breeding species from parts of England.

Nest
In hole at foot of wall, under tree stump, or in old rabbit burrow. Cup-shaped, built with grasses and moss, lined with hair and wool.

Eggs
Pale blue. Clutch 5-7.

Food
Insects, spiders, grubs, berries.

Ring Ouzel
Turdus torquatus

Ring Ouzel

Size and Field Characteristics   24 cm.
Slightly smaller than Blackbird. Sometimes called
Mountain Blackbird. Male has black plumage with paler
edges to feathers on wings and under-parts, distinct
white crescent on breast. Female has browner plumage
with fainter white crescent. As intolerant towards
humans as the Blackbird is tolerant.
Status
Summer resident.
Habitat and Range
Remote areas of hill, moorland and mountain with rocky
gullies and heathery slopes. Widespread throughout
British Isles except for south-west corner, breeding
confined to higher regions. Winters in Mediterranean
Region and North Africa.
Nest
Concealed on ground among heather, or on rocky ledge,
built with heather stalks, grasses and roots.
Eggs
Bluish-green with brownish markings. Clutch 4-6.
Food
Insects, worms, berries.

Dartford Warbler
Sylvia undata

Dartford Warbler

Size and Field Characteristics 12.5 cm.
Smaller than Chaffinch. Male has grey head, dark brown back and tail, noticeably long tail, dark reddish under-parts with white belly. Female is paler. Skulking habits, but male will ascend to topmost twig of gorse bush to sing.

Status
Resident.

Habitat and Range
Gorse and heather-covered heaths of southern England.

Nest
Built in low bush, with grasses and moss, lined with finer fibres.

Eggs
Off-white, heavily marked with yellowish-brown and grey. Clutch 3-4.

Food
Insects and spiders, making the Dartford Warbler vulnerable during severe winters.

Whitethroat
Sylvia communis

Whitethroat

Size and Field Characteristics 14 cm.
Slightly smaller than Chaffinch. Both sexes have
chestnut-brown wings, pale under-parts and distinct
white throats, male has grey head, female's is brown.

Status
Summer resident.

Habitat and Range
Frequents low scrub, hedge bottoms, wayside patches of
bramble and nettle, earning it the name of 'Nettle
Creeper'. Widespread throughout Britain, except for
Highlands and extreme north of Scotland. Winters in
Africa south of the Sahara.

Nest
A grassy cup lined with hair, built among brambles or
other dense vegetation.

Eggs
Pale olive spotted with grey. Clutch 4-6.

Food
Mainly insects.

Related Species
The Lesser Whitethroat (*Sylvia curruca*) slightly smaller
than Whitethroat having shorter tail. A shy bird, the
Lesser Whitethroat has greyer plumage than Whitethroat,
with no chestnut on the wings. The Lesser Whitethroat
nests at slightly higher levels and, though widespread
throughout most of England and Wales, is a rarity in
Scotland. Winters in Africa.

Carrion Crow
Corvus corone

Carrion Crow

Size and Field Characteristics   47 cm.
Slightly larger than Rook. Glossy black plumage, black legs and beak.
Status
Resident.
Habitat and Range
Hill moorland, farmland, woodland, town and city parks. Widespread throughout the whole of Britain except for north-west Scotland, where its place is taken by the Hooded Crow.
Nest
A strong bulky structure built with sticks, twigs, earth and wool, usually in hawthorn, conifer or other tree. In Hooded Crow territory many nests built on ground.
Eggs
Bluish-green, spotted with brown and grey. Clutch 3-5.
Food
Carrion of all kinds, small mammals, grain. Carrion and Hooded Crows are responsible for the destruction of many ground-nesting birds' eggs and young during the breeding season.
Related Species
The Hooded Crow differs from the Carrion Crow by having distinct grey mantle, breasts and under-parts. Where the ranges of the Carrion and Hooded Crow overlap the two may hybridize.

Raven
Corvus corax

Raven

Size and Field Characteristics   64 cm.
Larger than Rook. Largest member of the Crow family.
A huge black-plumaged bird with large beak and shaggy
throat feathers. Performs fantastic aerial evolutions
above breeding territory in early spring, twisting, diving
and flying upside down while uttering deep 'pruk-pruk'
call.
Status
Resident.
Habitat and Range
Sea cliffs, hilly and mountainous terrain, mainly on the
western half of the country.
Nest
Built on rocky ledge or fork of tree, a bulky construction
of sticks, heather stalks, moss, earth and wool. An
extremely durable nest.
Eggs
Bluish-green with brown and grey markings. Clutch 3-7.
Food
Small mammals, vegetable matter, with sheep carrion
forming most of diet in breeding season; thus decrease
in sheep farming accounts for noticeable decrease in
Raven population in some areas.

Yellowhammer
Emberiza citrinella

Yellowhammer

Size and Field Characteristics 16.5 cm.
Larger than Chaffinch. Male has bright yellow head and breast, brown streaked back and chestnut rump, longish dark tail. Female is much duller on the head and breast. Male sings from prominent perch on bush or telegraph wire in breeding territory. Flocks with other buntings and finches in winter and roosts communally in reed beds.

Status
Resident.

Habitat and Range
Farmland, heathland, scrubland and young conifer plantations throughout most of British Isles.

Nest
Built in low bush, conifer or on the ground, a bulky cup of grasses, moss and hair.

Eggs
Pale purplish, with dark spots and squiggles. Clutch 3-5.

Food
Insects, spiders, seeds.

Corn Bunting
Miliaria calandra

Corn Bunting

Size and Field Characteristics 18 cm.
Larger than Chaffinch. Largest and plainest of British
Buntings Light and dark-brown streaked upper-parts,
pale under-parts with dark spots on breast, large head
and stout bill. Perches prominently on telegraph wire,
fence or post in breeding territory, when song sounds
like the 'jangle of keys'. Legs may be seen to dangle in
short flights. Corn Buntings form flocks in winter.
Status
Resident.
Habitat and Range
Open fields of cereal crops on farmland throughout most
of England, scarcer in Scotland and rare in Wales.
Nest
On ground or close to it among growing corn, long grass
or low bramble.
Eggs
Greyish, marked with black spots and hair lines. Clutch
3-5.
Food
Weed seeds, grain, insects.

Reed Bunting
Emberiza schoeniclus

Reed Bunting

Size and Field Characteristics 15.5 cm.
Larger than Chaffinch. Male has brown and black
streaked upper-parts, grey rump, whitish under-parts,
white outer feathers to dark tail. In summer, male's
head is black with white collar and chin stripe. In
winter, head resembles that of duller female, brown and
grey. Male sings from prominent perch such as tall reed
stem in territory.
Status
Resident.
Habitat and Range
Open, damp, reedy areas, scrub, farmland and young
conifer plantations throughout the British Isles.
Nest
Situated low in reedy tussock or hedge bottom, built
with reeds, grasses and fine fibres.
Eggs
Olive-brown with black spots and squiggles. Clutch 4-5.
Food
Seeds, insects, caterpillars, occasionally visits bird tables
in winter.

Cirl Bunting
Emberiza cirlus

Cirl Bunting

Size and Field Characteristics 16.5 cm.
Larger than Chaffinch. Male has chestnut-streaked back
and dark tail, yellow under-parts with white undertail
feathers, greenish breast band. Striking black and yellow
face markings – best identification feature. Female
resembles female Yellowhammer, with greyish, not
chestnut, rump.
Status
Rare. Resident.
Habitat and Range
Limited to south and south-west England, where
overgrown hedgerows bordering farmland and bushy
hillsides are favoured habitat
Nest
Well-concealed, low in thick bush. Built with twigs,
grasses, moss and fine fibres.
Eggs
Greenish-blue, with brownish squiggles. Clutch 3-4.
Food
Mainly seeds and grain, insects.

Snow Bunting
Plectrophenax nivalis

Snow Bunting

Size and Field Characteristics 16 cm.
Larger than Chaffinch. A robust and attractive Bunting.
Male in summer, white head and body, black wings with
white patches, black and white tail. In winter, closely
resembles browner female. Snow Buntings may be
found in large flocks during winter months.

Status
Resident and winter visitor.

Habitat and Range
Small numbers of Snow Buntings breed on high Scottish
mountains. Large numbers from the high Arctic regions
winter in northern Britain and the east coast.

Nest
In crevice or hole under large stone, built with moss,
grasses, hair and feathers, usually feathers of Ptarmigan.

Eggs
Whitish with grey and brown markings. Clutch 4-7.

Food
Seeds, grain and insects.

Related Species
The Lapland Bunting (*Calcarius lapponicus*) is a rare
breeding bird of the northern Scottish mountains. More
often seen as a winter visitor from Scandinavia to the
east coast. In summer, male has brown streaked upper-
parts and distinct black head with white eye-stripe. In
winter, closely resembles chestnut-brown streaked
female.

Index